SCIENCE
SORTED/

Brains, bodies, guts and stuff

Glenn Murphy received his master's degree in science communication from London's Imperial College of Science, Technology and Medicine. He wrote his first popular science book, *Why Is Snot Green?*, while managing the Explainer team at the Science Museum in London. In 2007 he moved to the United States. He now lives and works in Raleigh, North Carolina, with his wife, Heather, and two unusually large and ill-tempered cats.

Favourite science fact: the eye of a colossal squid measures 27 cm (almost a foot) across. It has the largest eyes of any animal in the world.

SCIENCE SORTED

Brains, bodies, guts and stuff

By Glenn Murphy

Illustrated by Mike Phillips

MACMILLAN CHILDREN'S BOOKS

This book is produced in association with the Science Museum. Royalties from the sale of this product help fund the museum's exhibitions and programmes.

The Science Museum, London Internationally recognized as one of the world's leading science centres. It contains more than 10,000 amazing exhibits, two fantastic simulator rides and the astounding IMAX cinema. Enter a world of discovery and achievement, where you can see, touch and experience real objects and icons which have shaped the world we live in today or visit www.sciencemuseum.org.uk to find out more.

First published 2011 by Macmillan Children's Books

This edition published 2013 by Macmillan Children's Books
a division of Macmillan Publishers Limited
20 New Wharf Road, London N1 9RR
Basingstoke and Oxford
Associated companies throughout the world
www.panmacmillan.com

ISBN 978-1-4472-5137-8

Printed and bound by CPI Group (UK) Ltd, Croydon, CR0 4YY

Thanks to:

Gaby Morgan, Dom Kingston, Tracey Ridgewell, Fliss Stevens, Cee Weston-Baker and all at Macmillan Children's Books for their continuing support.

Deborah Patterson, Wendy Burford and everybody at the Science Museum who offered their help, support and comments.

Professor G. Neale, Clinical Safety Research Unit, Imperial College, London, for comments, corrections and marvellously helpful suggestions – all very much appreciated.

Dr Minou Pham for medical services rendered beyond the call of duty.

Dr Chris Martin and everyone at Martin Dental, Raleigh, for an all-new appreciation of teeth!

Dr Scot Schwichow (PhD, John Blaze Linguistics) and of course the lovely Diane.

Russ and Michelle Campbell, Brian and Stephanie Campbell, Richard and Juliette Oliveros, Brandon and Kristen Sommerfeld, and everyone at NCSystema for their invaluable friendship and support.

Norman and Marie Sudbury, and the whole extended Canadian clan (Lance, Toni, Jason, Vanessa, Justin, Serena and Matthew).

As always, Mum, Dad, the Murphs, the Witts, Heather, Kage and Austin. Big love to you all. x

Contents

Introduction

You are superhuman! If you think about it, you are pretty amazing.

Incredible, even. Your body is simply fantastic. In fact, I've never seen anything so impressive in all the biological world.

Hey, thanks! You know I do try to eat right, and get lots of fresh air. Plus I just had my hair cut, and this new zit cream really helps with—
Not just you – *everybody*.

Oh. Right. I knew that.
Or should I say every **body**.

The human body is just *beautifully* built. It's strong, it's supple, it's smart and it's agile. Inside, there's a stunning range of body systems which work together day in, day out, for years and years. The systems allow you to eat, breathe, run, jump, think, feel, heal broken bones, fight off diseases and more.

In this book, we'll be taking a trip through each of your body's systems. We'll explore bruising, bleeding, fainting and farting. We'll break bones and lose teeth. We'll find out why spinning makes you dizzy, where feelings come from and what double-jointed people look like on X-rays.

We'll do puzzles and quizzes. And we'll do

experiments on your brain(!).

By the end of it all, you'll *amaze* your friends and family with your new body of knowledge. (Or should that be 'knowledge of body'? Whatever.)

Sounds good. Where do we start?

Well, before we can explore what the body *does*, we have to understand how it's *made* and how it's *built*.

So how do we do that?

Simple. We build one for ourselves . . .

1. How to Build a Body

Okay, so let's imagine that you want to build a human body . . .

What, out of bits of dead people? Like Frankenstein or something?
No, not like that. You're not allowed to use whole arms, legs and heads. They're already half-built, aren't they? I meant a whole human body, built from *scratch*. Where would you start?

Hmmm . . . let's see. I s'pose I'd start with a skeleton. I'd wire a bunch of bones together, like they do with dinosaur bones in museums, and make a skeleton.
That's a good start. But a skeleton can't stand up or move by itself. You can dangle it from a hook to stop it collapsing into a heap of bones, but that's about it. How are going to get it standing and moving?

Easy. I strap some muscles on there. String 'em between all the bones, so they can hold the skeleton up and pull the arms and legs about. Oh, and then cover the whole lot with skin, so it doesn't look too hideous.
Nice work. This body is really starting to take shape. But here's the thing – if those muscles are

going to do any work at all, they'll need *energy*. Where are you going to get that?

Ah. Good point. Right, then – we stick in a stomach and some guts in it, so it can digest food, and get energy from that. Oh, and stick some teeth in the gob, so it can mash the food up. And a food tube, I s'pose, to get food from the mouth to the stomach.

Great idea. So now you've got a **digestive tube** for absorbing nutrients to feed the muscles. And, once you've got all the energy you can from your food, you can – ahem – 'drop' what's left out of the other end of the tube. Excellent.

Thank you.

But working muscles need *oxygen* too, otherwise they can't use the chemical food-energy you've just absorbed. Where are you going to get that?

Easy – shove some lungs in. And some air tubes leading

to the nose and mouth. Sorted.
Not quite.

Eh? (Sigh) What now?
Now you have two lungs full of oxygen, and a gut
full of chemical energy from your food. But how are
you going to get the oxygen and energy to muscles
spread all over your body, from head to toe?

**Oh, yeah. Hmmmm . . . tricky one, that. Hang
on . . . got it!**
On you go . . .

**You pipe the oxygen and energy there in little
blood tubes! You link all the muscles, guts, lungs
and stuff together with veins and arteries. Then
you stick a heart in the middle to pump the blood
around.**
Well done. You've created a **bloodstream**, which will
now carry oxygen and energy all over the body – a
brilliant solution. But there's still a problem. What's
going to keep the whole system working together?
How are you going to *coordinate* and *control* all this
eating, breathing, pumping and moving about?

**Doh! Of course! I forgot the brain! Okay – here's
what we do. We shove a brain in the skull to
control everything, and we wire it up to all the
body bits we already have with nerves. Oh, and**

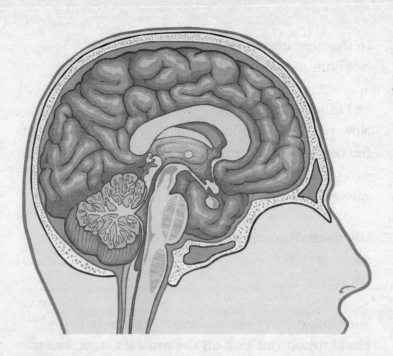

while we're about it let's stick some eyeballs and eardrums in the head too. And wire up the nose, mouth and skin so they can smell, taste and touch things. Howzat?

A masterstroke. Now your body can control itself and get information about the outside world through your five senses of sight, sound, touch, taste and smell. (And, as a bonus, your brain also lets you think and learn about stuff as you go.) We're nearly there.

Nearly?

Yep, nearly. Just a couple more things to deal with, and we're done. Now think hard, because this next one's a biggie.

You've just built a body using most of the major **organ systems** needed for life. You have a **movement** (or **musculoskeletal**) **system** made of bones and muscles. You have a **digestive system** for absorbing energy. You have a **breathing** (or **respiratory**) **system** for absorbing oxygen. You have a **blood** (or **circulatory**) **system** for moving the oxygen and energy around. And you have a **brain** and **nervous system** with which to control the whole lot. Now, what are you going to build all these organs and systems out of?

Errr . . . what?
Well, so far you've built a muscly skeleton, skin, guts, lungs, blood vessels, nerves, eyes, ears, a heart and a brain. What will you actually use to build these body organs? Wood? Plasticine? Lego? What?

Oh. Wow. I . . . errr . . . never thought about that. Well, bones are made of bone, aren't they? And muscles are made of . . . well . . . muscle?
That's right, they are. But it goes a bit deeper than that. In biology, we call these organ-building materials *tissues*. Most tissues are made of stringy **protein fibres**, **fatty membranes** and **watery, sugary gels**. Some special tissues, like bone tissue, also contain minerals like calcium, to make them tougher and stronger. But, for the most part, your tissues are woven from proteins, fats, sugars and water.

This is, of course, why you have to *eat* these things – your food isn't just for energy, it also provides the building blocks for body tissues – you literally *are* what you eat! Inside the body, proteins, fats and sugars are combined in hundreds of different ways to produce scores of different tissue types. But now we have a *new* problem.

What's that?
Now your body is *delicious and nutritious*. Proteins, fats and sugars aren't just good grub for us. They're also good grub for bacteria and other microscopic parasites – which just love to invade your body and munch away on your yummy tissues. Before long, your precious body will be chewed up, rotten and decayed. So how are you going to stop them?

Wrap yourself in cling film? Take some antibiotics?
Okay, not bad. In a way, your *skin* acts like cling film – covering your delicate, watery tissues with a protective layer that stops bacteria getting in. And while your body doesn't make antibiotics, it does make **antibodies** and other bacteria-busting defence systems, which lie in the tissues and bloodstream, waiting to do battle.

But even with all these defences your tissues will eventually break down by themselves. Just as cogs, wheels, circuits and pipes wear out inside machines, so too do your bones, joints, muscles, nerves and blood tubes. How are you going to fix that?

Errr . . . repair them? Or replace the worn-out parts with new ones?
Excellent. That's exactly what we'll do. In fact, we'll go one better. We'll make the tissues repair and regenerate themselves. As old parts wear down, we'll grow new parts to replace them.

We can do that? How?
By building our tissues out of living, growing, regenerating **cells**.

Cells are the most basic building blocks of life. The tissues of your body may be made of proteins, fats and sugars, but they're organized into tissues by layers of cells. Muscle tissue is built with layers of muscle cells, bone tissue with bone cells, brain and nerve tissue with nerve cells. And so on.

But don't cells wear out too?
Most of them do, yes. But cells also grow and divide, replacing layers of old, dead cells in a tissue with fresh, new ones from beneath. Inside the nucleus (or command centre) of each cell, instructions coded into DNA are decoded and used to direct the assembly of cells into tissues.

As your tissues age and wear down, the healthy cells within them grow and divide to replace the ageing ones (which conveniently self-destruct). In this way, old blood, skin, nerve, muscle and bone cells are shed (or passed) from your body every day, each one replaced by a shiny new cell. In the absence of a nasty disease or accident, the whole process keeps your body ticking along for decades, with no mechanic, plumber or electrician required. Let's see any other machine top that!

So that's it, then? We've done it? We've built a body?

Yep – we're done.

Hooray! We rule!

Good job. We now have a living, breathing, moving body that can take care of itself. We've used cells to build tissues, tissues to build organs and organs to build organ systems. Now just add food, water and oxygen, and you're away!

Now you understand how the body is built, you're ready to explore the really *good* stuff. In the chapters that follow, we'll tackle the body system by system, and discover why we sweat, why we itch and why we have toes. We'll find out how farts become eggy, how karate masters chop through concrete, and how you could live with half a brain.

You ready, Dr Frankenstein?

Then let's do it . . .

2. Blood, Breath and Body Pumps

How do babies breathe before they're born?
They don't. Because they don't have to. While they're in the womb, their mothers do their breathing for them. And while babies do 'practise' breathing in the womb, they don't take their first breath until they're pushed out into the cold, airy world.

What? Babies don't breathe? But how is that possible? Wouldn't they suffocate?
Nope. They do just fine. They get all the oxygen they need from their mothers, so they don't need to breathe. At least not until they're out of the womb and the **umbilical cord** that connects them to their mothers is cut.

So they breathe through that tube? Like a snorkel or something?
In a manner of speaking, yes. Only they're not actually breathing. They're just receiving oxygen through the cord, and making use of it.

I don't get it. If you stop breathing, you die. Everybody knows that.
Ah, but that's not strictly true, you see. At least not for everybody, all the time. Think about it – how

long can you hold your breath?

I dunno – about a minute?
Right. And did you die last time you tried?

Don't be stupid. If I did, I couldn't say so, could I?
Exactly. So you stopped breathing for a full minute and yet here you are, alive and well.

Eh? So you're saying that babies hold their breath? For, like, nine months?
No, no, no, no, no. Not at all. I'm saying that you don't necessarily have to be breathing to be receiving and using oxygen. That's because there's a big difference between **breathing** (moving air in and out of your lungs) and **respiration** (using oxygen from your bloodstream to power your brain and other tissues). If you stop respiring, your cells cannot use oxygen to power

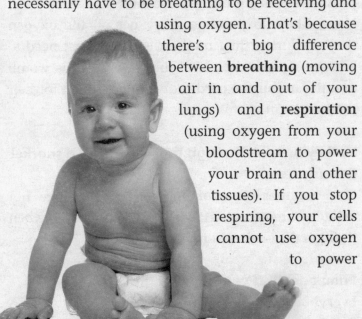

themselves, and you die. But you can stop **breathing** for several minutes before you stop **respiring**. That's why you can hold your breath without dying. What's more, if you can find another way to get oxygen into your bloodstream, then you don't need to breathe at all.

So how do babies do it?

For the nine months that it's inside the womb, a baby (or rather, the **foetus***) receives oxygen through the **umbilical cord**. This fleshy cord is made up of three thick blood vessels (two **umbilical arteries** and one **umbilical vein**). The umbilical vein passes into the foetus's belly (where the navel or belly button will eventually be), and carries nutrients and fresh oxygen to the baby's liver and heart. On the return route, carbon dioxide and other wastes are carried from the baby's hip (or iliac) arteries, up past the bladder and back out through the belly into the umbilical veins. In this way, oxygen and nutrients pass in and out of the body of the growing foetus without it ever having to breathe (or, for that matter, eat).

PLACENTA

UMBILICAL CORD

VEIN

ARTERIES

---

* This is the correct word for a baby developing in the womb, before it is actually born.

So where does the umbilical cord come from? From the mother's blood?

Not directly, no. Mixing the mother's blood and the baby's blood would be dangerous, as it could expose the foetus to all sorts of viruses, bacteria or toxic chemicals, against which it has no defence. So, instead, blood vessels from the mother and from the foetus meet inside the womb, within a special organ called the **placenta**. The placenta is formed from the same fertilized egg the foetus developed from, and it floats beside the foetus in the womb. Inside the placenta, capillaries from the mother's bloodstream and from the foetus's umbilical cord twine around each other like a pair of hands with interlacing fingers.

Arranged in this way, oxygen and nutrients can move back and forth through the spaces between the two bloodstreams without them ever actually flowing into each other. So the placenta works like a fleshy sieve, filtering out any nasties before they get into the umbilical cord and the foetus's blood. Which is pretty nifty, if you think about it.

So the baby doesn't use its lungs at all?

Not really, no. Right up until it's born, the foetus's lungs are filled with fluid. From about three months onwards, it makes small breathing movements with the lungs. But it's not really using the lungs to breathe with at all – it's just preparing the breathing muscles for use later on. Like a breathing 'workout' inside the womb.

But if the lungs were filled with fluid, wouldn't the baby drown when it tried to use them?
Well spotted. It *would*, but it *doesn't*. Right after the baby is pushed out of the womb, it gives a mighty heave, coughs up all the fluid, and starts breathing with its first cry (doctors, nurses and midwives sometimes hold the baby upside down and pat it gently on the back to help kick-start this first breath once the baby is delivered). That's why the first thing the baby does is cry. Well – that, and because it's chilly and scary out in the big, bad world.

Wow. That's kind of amazing. Okay – one more thing. What happens to the umbilical cord and the placenta?
Once the baby is born and breathing for itself, the umbilical cord starts to shrivel up. If left alone, it would eventually break off all by itself, but in practice doctors usually clamp it and cut it a few centimetres from the baby's belly to speed this process up. The rest of it is pulled back inside the baby's abdominal cavity, to form the belly button.

As for the placenta, that pops out – attached to the other end of the umbilical cord – right after the baby. Usually the nurses just throw it away, but sometimes the parents decide to keep it as a souvenir.

Ewwww! That's gross!!
You think *that's* icky? Some parents even . . . No, I shouldn't say. It's probably too much for you.

What? Come on, tell me. What could be worse than keeping it as a souvenir?
Okay, you asked for it. Some parents fry it up and eat it.

(Bleurrrghh!)

Why do big cuts need stitches?

Because although your skin has an amazing ability to repair itself, wide or deep cuts take much longer to heal. Stitches help to hold the edges of the wound together, and keep the wound sealed off to nasty bacteria while your body gets to work patching you up.

So why do bigger ones need sewing up? Is it so you won't bleed to death?

Not really, no. Usually all the bleeding has stopped by the time the surgeon or nurse starts to stitch the edges of a wound together. If it *hasn't* stopped, then stitching you up won't do much good anyway, as you'll continue to bleed into the muscles and other tissues beneath the skin. Even with no blood leaking from your body, you could still bleed to death as the blood leaks and pools inside your leg or stomach and fails to reach your brain.

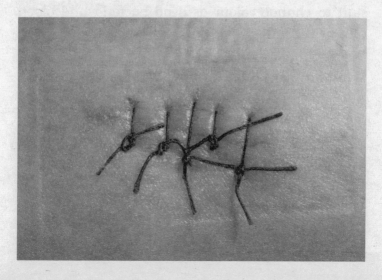

But if you get a little cut, your skin heals up all by itself. So why do only bigger cuts need stitches? What do you mean?

Well, let's say I'm at home playing with my cat, and she scratches me on the back of the hand. How does it work?

Well, with smaller cuts – like scratches – bleeding stops very quickly. As soon as your kitty's claws separate the skin, your body senses the injury, and blood vessels close to the wound shrink up to slow blood flow to the area. Then a blood clot quickly forms and plugs the small gap across the scratch. Once the bleeding has stopped, the clot then turns into one or more scabs, which appear on your skin as dark, crusty lines. Beneath the scabs, the blood vessels open again to allow bacteria-busting white blood cells to move from the bloodstream into the broken tissues of the scratch. They kill all the bacteria, and the scabs start to change colour as dead bacteria and blood cells beneath them pile up.

What happens after that?
After that, special cells deep within your skin, called fibroblasts, start to multiply and grow from each side of the cut towards the middle, forming a new layer of skin beneath the scab. If all goes well, the new skin will be fully formed within a day or two, and the scabs will fall off to reveal clean, fresh skin and no

trace at all of your mean kitty's scratches.

Okay. So *now* let's say I'm at the zoo. A huge tiger escapes, and he comes running right at me . . .
O-kay . . .

. . . at the last second, I hold up my backpack, hoping he'll prefer the sausage sandwiches in my lunch box to eating me alive. Rrrrrrrooowwwlll! He swipes it out of my hands, and I run away. But his claws have sliced a massive, nasty cut right along the length of my arm, and it's gushing blood all over the place. *Now* what?
Well, that's all very dramatic – if a little scary.

Thank you. I try my best. So what happens now?
Well, obviously a deep gash carved out by a tiger's claw won't heal up nearly as easily as a little swipe from Tiddles. This time the cut will go through more layers of skin, probably into the fibrous tissue and muscle below. And the gap it creates can't easily be plugged and bridged by blood clots and fibroblasts. Presuming that you made it to a hospital, or got some emergency medical help, the doctor or paramedic would try to stop the bleeding by binding the arm tightly with bandages that press down hard on to the cut. This pressure might create a temporary clot and, just as before, the blood vessels near the wound would shrink up (or constrict) to slow blood loss from

the area. But, left as it is, this bigger, deeper wound would probably not heal by itself.

Why not?
Well, the clot – if it formed at all – would probably fall apart as soon as you removed the bandages* to clean the wound, and you would continue bleeding. And even if another clot formed, it wouldn't hold for long. With too big a gap across the wound, the fibroblasts that make new skin and muscle tissue would be unable to meet in the middle and seal off the wound. So clots and scabs would keep breaking up and falling out of the wound. The gash would ooze blood and pus, and eventually it would become infected by bacteria. Before long your whole arm would be infected, and surgeons would have to remove it to stop the bacteria infecting the rest of your body and killing you.

Ugh! Nasty!
Yep. So to avoid this – and to give your body a hand with the healing process – a doctor would remove the bandages, clean the wound with anti-bacterial chemicals, bring the edges of the wound together and finally sew (or staple) them up. With less of a gap to bridge, the blood clots and scabs should hold for longer, buying enough time for the fibroblasts to

---

* If you *didn't* remove the bandages, bacteria from the air (or the tiger's claws) would grow beneath them and infect the wound.

regrow new tissue underneath.

Then it'd heal up again? Good as new?
No, not quite. With a deeper cut and a wider gap to bridge, the fibroblasts have to use emergency repair tactics to make sure it holds together. So instead of new skin tissue – complete with nerves, blood vessels, hair follicles and sweat glands – they weave the wound together with dense mats of a tough protein called collagen. What's left is a patch of pale, hairless, dead-feeling **scar tissue**. This patch of your arm would never tan or sweat beneath the sun, and would look different from the rest of your skin for life. But hey – at least you didn't get infected. Or eaten.

All right, what if you were attacked by a ninja assassin and he chopped your arm right off?
That would be tougher. If you could stop the bleeding, pick up your arm and get straight to a hospital, there would be a chance that a surgeon could reattach it. This is much easier to do with fingers and toes than entire arms or legs. But this has been done many times before (not so much the ninja attack – I mean people getting limbs chopped off by harvesting machines and having them

reattached – stuff like that). And although it leaves lots of scar tissue, sometimes people can keep using the arm for life afterwards.

What about if your whole head got chopped off?
Well . . . even if a surgeon *could* stop the bleeding and reattach your head with an operation (which, at present, is pretty much impossible), it would take hours to do it. And since your brain can't survive for more than a few *minutes* without a blood supply, I wouldn't fancy your chances.

Oh. So I should definitely avoid angry tigers and ninjas, then.
Yes. I'd say that was good advice, anyway . . .

Puzzle: blood-clot boggle

Now you're an expert on blood clots, try this jumbled-up picture-puzzle. In your head, assemble the five pictures in the correct order, so that when you read them from left to right, you have a comic strip telling the story of how blood clots are created. What order do the pictures appear in? Check your answers on page 234.

If your blood didn't clot, would you die from a paper cut?

Yes, you would. Although it would take a while, since paper cuts only sever small blood vessels, and it would still take several days to drip-bleed to death. In reality though, this could never happen because if your blood didn't clot at all you wouldn't live long enough to get cut in the first place.

Eh? You've lost me there. You mean if your blood didn't clot, you'd never get cut?
No, I'm not saying *that*. I'm saying that if you were born without the ability to form blood clots – at all – then you'd be lucky to survive more than a few weeks, let alone long enough to be leafing through books and magazines and getting paper cuts. Even haemophiliacs have *some* ability to form clots, otherwise they'd never make it through birth and early childhood.

Hang on – what's a haemophiliac when it's at home?
Haemophilia is a blood disorder in which the blood fails to form complete clots, or forms clots less easily than it should. This puts people who suffer from the disease – called haemophiliacs – in great danger when they are injured. For a haemophiliac, even very light bumps and falls can cause bleeding beneath

the skin – especially into joints. And if they're badly hurt, such as breaking a leg on the football pitch or breaking ribs in a car crash, then their internal injuries can be life-threatening.

That doesn't sound too good. So how do you get it? Can you catch it?
No, you can't catch it. Basically, you're born with it. You inherit the disorder from one or both of your parents. It's caused by faulty genes, which fail to produce one or more of the many proteins in your bloodstream (called clotting factors) that make blood clotting possible.

Clots are made by proteins? I thought maybe they were stored somewhere in the body – like a warehouse full of bathplugs, and got whisked in to plug up the holes whenever you got pricked or cut.
Not quite. Instead, an injury activates one protein, which changes shape and activates another. Then that protein does the same to another one, and so on, and so on. At the end of it all, a clot is formed. But there are more than twenty different proteins and steps along the way. And, if any one of them fails, the clot doesn't form correctly, or fails to form at all.

Think of it this way. The proteins – blood-clotting factors – are like little spies. They're everywhere, unseen, keeping an eye on things and just waiting to jump into action. They float throughout the entire body in the bloodstream, watching the walls of your skin and other tissues, keeping an eye out for gaps.

Gaps? What kind of gaps?

Any break in the tissues, large or small, that could let your precious blood cells go rushing out or that could let in the army of invading bacteria waiting outside the walls. So the little spies keep a constant eye out for danger, and report back to spy HQ in the brain. When you're injured and the walls are breached, blood cells start to rush out. The first of the spies sense this and some of them, called **platelets**, respond by clumping together to form a weak, temporary plug.

They also signal other spies, which change their shape and appearance (like putting on a false moustache), and contact more moustachioed spies to spread the word about the injury. A clump of them forms a **platelet plug**. Then the moustache spies change shape too (let's say they put on some sunglasses and a small black hat) and contact more

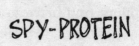

SPY-PROTEIN

spies. And so it goes on, until eventually the word gets to a gang of burly, hat-and-shades-wearing, moustachioed builder proteins called **fibrinogens**.

These builders then start grabbing blocks of another protein (called **fibrin**) from all around them, and use these blocks to build a more solid wall. This wall of fibrin (called a **fibrin plug**) replaces the flimsy platelet one that went before it, and seals up the gap to stop the blood getting out (and the bacteria getting in). Along the way, some of the spies signal Spy HQ in the brain. The brain responds by sending bacteria-battling white-blood-cell reinforcements to the injury site (just in case a few got in), followed by instructions to starting the healing process.*

Whew! That's quite a battle! Why is it all so complicated?

The many steps and chains of proteins are there to prevent false alarms. If you think about it, you wouldn't want blood clots forming where you didn't actually need them. Blood clots that slip into the heart or brain can cause heart attacks or strokes. If clotting happened in one quick step, then every bump or knock could trigger a clot that might accidentally kill you. So having lots of protein 'spies' confirm the injury and activate each other helps to ensure the

---

* See 'Why do big cuts need stitches?' on page 17 for more about what happens next.

threat is real before they begin the drastic step of building a clot.

So what about the haemophiliacs? Are they missing a few protein spies or something?

More often, some of the proteins are the wrong shape. So it's as if some of their spies are wearing the wrong outfits, and can't recognize each other to pass on the message.

So they *could* die from getting a paper cut or something?

No. As I said, even haemophiliacs have some clotting ability. Their spies tend to be out of shape, but not absent altogether. So they might form a partial clot but not a whole one, or a temporary plug but not a permanent one. Which means they can happily survive shaving and paper cuts, but they might need special life-saving treatment if they're more seriously hurt. If *none* of your clotting factors work, and no clot forms at all, then you're unlikely even to survive being born.

Life is a rough-and-tumble business, and even birth involves being squeezed and pushed out of a womb. After that, you stumble and fall about as a toddler, you run, jump, tumble and play as a child, and suffer at least some bumps and bruises as an active adult. Every bump and bruise we get is actually a mini-clot protecting our tissues. Most of us don't realize the hundreds of little injuries, clots and repairs we go through each week, as our bodies just get on with it.

Wow. Life is tough. I'm glad my little spies are on the job.
Me too. Life would be a lot tougher without them . . .

Why do bruises change colour?

A bruise is a patch of damaged blood vessels beneath the skin. As these broken tubes leak blood into the surrounding area, it goes red or purple as it fills with dark red blood. Later, the bruise changes colour as the blood cells break down and the tubes are repaired.

So a bruise is really a little pool of blood under the skin?

Yep. Bruises – also known as **contusions** or **minor haematomas** – are areas of injured tissue beneath the skin. They form after you receive a bump or whack hard enough to bust open the little blood vessels that lie beneath the skin.

Like arteries and veins?

No, busting open large arteries and veins would lead to far worse problems than bruising.* Besides, arteries and veins are pretty tough to burst, and most arteries sit deep inside your arms, legs and torso, protecting them from impact. Bruises are usually the result of broken capillaries and venules. These are the tiny outer branches of your circulatory system, which run throughout your skin and muscle tissue and surround

---

* Busted arteries and veins cause **major haematomas**, which can be very dangerous, especially if the artery is in your head or neck. That's why it's so important to wear a helmet when you ride a bike.

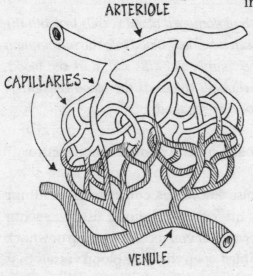

ARTERIOLE

CAPILLARIES

VENULE

your bones and internal organs.

While blood is pumped to and from the heart through arteries and veins, these wide vessels branch into narrower and narrower tubes as they make their way through your body. So the oxygen and nutrients in your blood travel first through **arteries**, then into much narrower **arterioles**, and finally to tiny webs of hair-like **capillaries**. There, oxygen and sugars are exchanged for carbon dioxide and other wastes, which travel back through more capillaries, then into wider **venules**, and finally into the fat **veins** that make their way back to the heart and lungs.

So when you get a nasty whack, the capillaries break open and leak blood everywhere?

Not everywhere, just into the immediate area. How wide an area depends on the toughness (or tone) of your skin and muscle tissue, and on how hard you were whacked. But, in any case, the area fills with red blood cells and plasma (the liquid bit of blood), making it swell and go red.

But bruises aren't red, they're blue or brown.
Right. That's because your body immediately sets about repairing the damage. It signals special cells to patch up the broken capillaries and others to clean up the spillage. As the spilt red blood cells break down, the **haemoglobin** protein inside (which gives them their red colour) breaks down into another protein call **haemosiderin**, which is greenish-brown in colour. Depending on how deep the bruise is beneath the veil of your skin, this can make it appear black, brown or blue.

But you get other colours too, right? So what do all the colours mean?
Right. Bruises can turn greenish or yellowish before they disappear altogether. The colours don't really 'mean' anything at all. They're just different colours produced as the haemoglobin and haemosiderin are broken down and removed by white blood cells.*

---

* That said, me and my mates at school used to score our bruises based on colour, just like in snooker. So you got 2 points for yellow, 3 points for green, 4 points for brown, and 7 points for black. The losers had to buy sweets for the winner each week. It certainly made footy injuries more interesting in winter.

Why do some people bruise more easily than others? I mean, old people get bruises all the time, right?

That's true, they do. Sometimes 'easy bruising' can be a sign of a blood disorder like **haemophilia.**[*] But even healthy people differ in how easily they bruise. It can depend on the condition of your skin, muscle and fibrous tissues, on your blood circulation, a lack of certain vitamins (like vitamin K) in your diet, and more. Women tend to bruise more easily than men because their skin tends to be thinner, and the fat layers protecting the blood vessels are arranged a little differently. Also, elderly people tend to bruise a lot more easily than younger people. This is because your skin gets thinner and the walls of your blood vessels gets weaker as you age.

So what should you do if you get a bruise?

If it's a light bump, just rubbing the area right after you've been injured can be enough to break up the swelling and stop a bruise from forming. If it's a pretty nasty bump (but still not a serious injury, which will always require a trip to the hospital), then the best thing to do is put an ice pack on it for ten to twenty minutes. If it's on your arm or leg, keep the limb raised above the level of your shoulders or hips

---

* See 'If your blood didn't clot, would you die from a paper cut?' on page 23 for more about this.

as you do so. This will slow down the leakage from your busted capillaries, and stop the bruise getting too big. Then eat plenty of fish and leafy green veg so that you get the vitamins you need to heal the bruise quickly.

No, I mean how can I *make* the bruise come out, so I can score maximum points?
Oh. Well, in that case, just leave your body to do its job. And take pictures of your bruise every day, so you get points for every colour it goes.

Genius! Thanks!
I aim to please.

Why do some people faint at the sight of blood?

Fainting happens when your blood pressure drops quickly and the brain is suddenly starved of oxygen. People may 'pass out' for all kinds of reasons, including pain, hunger, fear or poor blood circulation. But fainting at the sight of blood may be an ancient reflex that prevents you from bleeding to death.

Is passing out the same as getting knocked out?

No, not really. Both of them make you collapse and lose consciousness, but they happen in quite different ways. When you hit your head and get knocked out, the brain is shaken, rattled or crushed against the inside of the skull, causing temporary damage. In response, your brain immediately shuts down non-essential parts (like the motor regions that help you activate your muscles and stay standing) and puts you to sleep while it attempts emergency repairs.

So how is passing out any different?

Passing out – or fainting – happens when there's a sudden drop in blood pressure and/or oxygen supply to the brain. Very quickly, your brain senses this and shuts down non-essential parts so that it can survive longer without being damaged. Again, you lose consciousness and fall down as skeletal muscles are deactivated. But while knockouts almost always involve some form of brain damage, fainting usually does not. So being knocked out is a response to *actual* brain damage, while passing out is a response to the *threat* of brain damage.

But what could make your blood pressure drop like that?

Well, there are two ways it can happen. The first is when the total volume of blood in your body decreases for some reason. If you severed a limb or an artery, this would happen quite quickly as blood came pumping out of your body. The average adult has about 4–7 litres of blood in their body. Losing just 1–2 litres would be enough to make most people pass out (losing 2.5 litres or more would be enough to kill you).

But your total blood volume can drop even without any bleeding. If you don't eat or drink for a day or two, your blood pressure drops as you gradually use up water in your body, losing it through sweat, tears, breath (as water vapour), urine and faeces. Within three to five days,* your blood volume and pressure will drop low enough to make you pass out, repeatedly. And if you don't find water fast then eventually you won't wake up at all.

Usually, though, fainting and passing out happen

---

* This depends on how hot you are, and your body type. See 'How long could you survive without food or water?' on page 75 for more details.

for far less drastic reasons. When you faint through fear, pain or the sight of blood, it's not because you've suddenly lost lots of blood. It happens because the blood you *have* fails – at least temporarily – to reach your brain.

Eh? I don't get it. How?
Think of it this way. Imagine that your body is a big, plastic water bottle, filled to the top with lovely, red blood.

O-kayyyy . . .
Now, in order to stay conscious, the blood has to touch the cap at the top (your brain). This is fine as long as you're all topped up. But obviously, if you make a hole in the bottle, the liquid level will soon drop away from the cap (or brain) and you will pass out. A large hole will do this quickly, but making tiny pinholes to 'pee' or 'sweat' the liquid out will eventually have the same effect, right?

But what if, when the blood couldn't quite reach the top, you were allowed to squeeze the sides of the bottle, making the volume of the blood-holding vessel smaller?

Well, then the blood would be squeezed up the neck of the bottle, and it'd still touch the cap.
Exactly. And this, in a way, is what blood vessels do inside your body. By keeping the volume of the

container small, they keep the pressure up, and make sure that enough blood still reaches the brain up top.

But when you experience a sudden pain or fear, your body may respond by slowing your heart rate and widening the blood vessels in many parts of your body. This takes the 'squeeze' off the sides of the 'bottle', and your blood drops away from your brain to pool up in your legs. While some pressure remains in the upper body, it's not enough to feed the brain. So it responds by passing out, or fainting. This lays you out flat, so the blood can flow sideways (rather than upwards) and more easily reach your brain. Like turning our water-filled bottle on its side, so that the water swishes towards the cap under gravity alone.

But what good would that do you if you were scared or in pain?

Well, this 'pass-out' reflex may have evolved to help you 'play dead' when suddenly attacked by a much stronger animal. The idea is that the attacker may then just ignore you, and you live to fight another day. This is called the **vasovagal response**, and people can be more or less sensitive to it. So some people faint at the slightest pain or surprise, while others can endure incredible amounts of pain or shock before passing out.

Okay . . . I get that, I s'pose. But what about fainting at the sight of blood?

That may have once been a self-defence reflex too. If you're wounded and bleeding, passing out drops your heart rate and keeps you still. This helps slow the flow of blood from the wound, buying time for your blood to form a clot. Of course, that's only helpful if it's *you* that's bleeding. Passing out at the sight of *someone else's* blood is a pretty useless response, and mostly happens in people whose vasovagal responses are too sensitive. So the same folks who pass out easily when surprised or hurt are also likely to be floored by seeing you cut your finger.

Game: pass-out

Grab some plasticine and a plastic water bottle, and you can simulate passing out for yourself, just like we talked about here. Here's how you do it:

1. Grab a plastic bottle and fill it almost to the top with water.
2. Grab a ball of plasticine and sculpt a self-portrait (just the head, not the whole body).
3. For dramatic effect add a few drops of red food colouring to each bottle.
4. Put the cap on the bottle and stick the plasticine head on top.

5. Squeeze the sides of your bottle until the liquid touches the top. All the time there is liquid touching the cap, your 'head' is supplied with blood and you stay conscious. If you let go of the bottle, the pressure drops and your bottle person will faint.

Which works harder, your heart or your brain?

That kind of depends on whether you're busy thinking or busy exercising. Your heart works up to three times harder during exercise, and shifts enough blood over a lifetime to fill a supertanker. But, in the long run, your brain probably tips it. Because even when you're sitting still your brain is using twice as much energy as your heart, and it takes four to five times as much blood to feed it.

You mean your heart and brain actually eat blood? Like vampires or something?

Errr . . . not quite. It's more like they eat oxygen and glucose. All your organs do. Blood is just the conveyer belt that delivers these goodies to your hungry cells, tissues and organs. As we've already learned, red blood cells act like oxygen postmen. They pick up oxygen molecules in the lungs and carry them to hungry tissues throughout the body.

Glucose, meanwhile, moves into your bloodstream from the digestive system, and simply dissolves into your blood, making it slightly sweet and sugary. From there, it's carried around the body and dissolves into cells wherever it's needed.

OXYGEN POSTMAN

Like the muscles and the brain?

Right. While all your tissues use oxygen and glucose, your muscles and brain are perhaps the most ravenous. At rest, your muscles use around 15 per cent of your blood flow, while your brain uses roughly 20 per cent. Your heart, too, needs about 4–5 per cent of your blood supply, just to keep pumping. Without the constant movement of blood that your heart provides, your tissues would quickly become starved of oxygen and glucose, and your oxygen-hungry brain would begin to shut down. So your heart must work hard, and tirelessly, throughout your entire life.

So how hard does your heart pump?

At an average rate of 5.2 litres per minute. In one day (twenty-four hours), your heart pumps enough blood to fill the water tanks of *four* full-sized fire engines. Over a lifetime, the average heart pumps over 180 million litres of blood, or enough to fill an ocean-going oil supertanker!

Whoa! It's a good thing our bodies don't leak, isn't it?

Indeed. And that's nothing. During exercise, your tissues – especially your muscles – use up oxygen and glucose* much more quickly. In this state, your

---

* In doing so, they also create waste – such as carbon dioxide and lactic acid – more quickly too.

muscles need four or five times more blood than they did at rest, so the heart has to pump much harder and faster to meet the demand for more blood. When you're resting or sleeping, your heart beats at around sixty to a hundred times per minute. But when you're sprinting or swimming as fast as you can, your heart rate can reach 200 beats* per minute or more!

Oh, come on. Then your heart *has* to be working harder than the brain, right?
For short bursts, perhaps, yes. But, if you think about it, most of us sleep for a third of our lives, and spend very little time exercising this hard. Even for Olympic athletes, it's pretty much impossible to keep that level of exercise up for more than thirty minutes, let alone all day. So over the course of your lifetime your brain wins the prize.

In an average lifetime, the heart beats around 2 billion times and uses 7–10 per cent of the energy you consume through food. Now compare that with the brain, which uses around 20–25 per cent of your energy every day every week, and every year of your life – whether you're sprinting, sleeping or

---

* The average maximum heart rate decreases with age. You can figure yours out by subtracting your age from 220. So if you're ten years old, it's around 210 beats per minute. But when you reach forty, it tops out at about 180.

doing a Sudoku puzzle.*

So if my teacher tells me to 'use my brain', I can just take a nap in class and leave a note stuck to my head that says 'I am!' Brilliant!

Errr... you *could*, I suppose. But I wouldn't recommend it...

Experiment: see your heart beat!

You don't need fancy hospital gear to see your heartbeat in action. Try this:

1. Grab a small, pea-sized blob of plasticine or clay, a stopwatch and a matchstick.
2. Stick the matchstick most of the way through the clay blob.
3. Rest your arm, palm up, on a table in front of you.
4. Stick the clay blob on to the inside of your wrist, just below the base of the thumb.
5. You should see the match twitch as it picks up the movement of the blood pulsing through the blood vessel beneath. If it's not moving, unstick the blob and try shifting it a little to the left or right. Got it? Good.

---

* To put it another way, if the average European or American eats about 60 tonnes of food in a lifetime, then roughly 6 tonnes of it fuel the heart while 15 tonnes are devoured by the hungry brain.

6. Now take the stopwatch, set it to beep after one minute, and count how many times the match twitches before it goes off. (If you don't have a stopwatch, get a friend to time it with an ordinary watch – you just count heartbeats, and your friend tells you when a minute is up.)

7. How many 'beats' did you count? The average for an adult is sixty to eighty beats per minute; for children, it's eighty to a hundred.

8. Now remove the blob and do two minutes of non-stop exercise. You can do pushups, sit-ups, hop, skip, jump, jog on the spot – whatever. Just keeping going for two full minutes.

9. Reattach the blob and matchstick, and count the beats per minute as before.

10. How high did your heart rate go? Compare your score with your friends, and draw up a table showing your heart rates after exercise. The winner (or the fittest person) is the one with the *lowest* score!

Why don't lungs work underwater?

Because they didn't evolve to move liquids in and out. And, even if they could, it still wouldn't work. Water contains far less free oxygen than air, so even if your lungs could inhale and exhale water they still couldn't get enough oxygen out to sustain your big, warm-blooded body.

But there's loads of oxygen in water. I mean, fish breathe underwater, right?

Right. But fish use gills to do it, not lungs. Gills are thin, feathery organs adapted for underwater breathing (or rather, underwater **respiration**), which are clearly visible on either side of the head. They have a huge surface area for capturing the oxygen dissolved in water and dumping carbon dioxide back into it. In fish respiration, water is moved past these surfaces by the movement of the gills, and the movement of the fish itself as it swims through the water.

Lungs, on the other hand, are found deep inside the body, further away from the oxygen source they need to get at. With each inhalation, air is sucked in through the nose or mouth and travels down your windpipe (or **trachea**). In the middle of your chest, the trachea splits into two major branches (or **bronchi**) which each enter a lung.

You have two big branches poking into your lungs? Yikes! Isn't that a bit dangerous?

Not *real* branches, no. More like *forks*.

What? Now you've got *cutlery* in there?
Errr . . . no. I meant 'branches' or 'forks' in the air tubes that lead into your lungs. As in 'junctions'. Okay?

Phew! That's a relief. Thought I was going to have to call an ambulance or something . . .
No, it's fine. You're fine. I'm fine. Now, where was I?

Airways?
Right. Airways. So, inside the lungs, these airways branch again and again into smaller and smaller passages called **bronchioles**. The whole thing looks a bit like an upside-down tree, with a trunk at the top and limbs and branches spreading out sideways into each lung. At the tips of these branches are tiny, berry-like sacs called **alveoli**. These sacs are lined with a thick layer of fluid, and surrounded by tiny blood vessels. Once it reaches the alveoli, oxygen from the air you inhale dissolves into the fluid inside, and oxygen and carbon dioxide are exchanged with red blood cells in the bloodstream. This done, the carbon dioxide dissolves out of the fluid, flows up through the bronchioles to the trachea, and exits the body as you exhale.

Aha! There you go, you see? The oxygen in your

lungs has to dissolve into the fluid in those little lung-berry things anyway, right? So why can't you just fill your lungs with water and let the oxygen from the

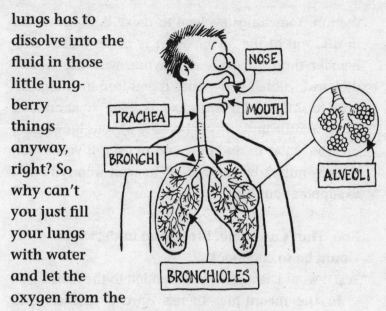

NOSE

MOUTH

TRACHEA

BRONCHI

ALVEOLI

BRONCHIOLES

water dissolve straight into the blood?

Well, if your lungs do happen to fill with water – as in when you're drowning – that's exactly what does happen.

Great! But wait – why do you drown, then?

Because unfortunately there just isn't anywhere near enough oxygen in a lungful of water for your body to get by. While there is some oxygen dissolved in fresh water, compared with air, the same volume of water contains twenty times less of it. Now that may be enough to sustain a cold-blooded fish with the right gear to extract it, but it's nowhere near enough oxygen for a large warm-blooded mammal like you.

And, besides, you don't have the right gear for

the job. Your lungs evolved to move light, gassy air in and out of the body. Water is much thicker and heavier than air, so – as anyone who has nearly drowned will tell you – once it gets into the lungs it's hard to shift, and it tends to stay there. In short, you can't breathe underwater because a) your lungs can't breathe water in and out, and b) even if you could, there wouldn't be enough air in each watery breath to support your body.

Boo. That's a shame. Breathing underwater would be so cooooool.
Yes, it would. But it's a skill best left to the fishes.

In the meantime, there's always snorkels and scuba gear . . .

If blood is red, why are veins blue?

Actually, veins are not blue at all. They're more of a clear, yellowish colour. And although blood looks red when it's outside the body, when it's sitting in a vein near the surface of the skin, it's more of a dark maroon colour. At the right depth, these blood-filled veins reflect less red light than the surrounding skin, making them look blue by comparison.

Hang on – that's not right. Veins aren't yellow, they're blue. Everybody knows that.

Well, 'everybody' has got it wrong, I'm afraid. Although some veins may look blue beneath the skin, if you remove them from the body and drain them of blood, they're more of a clear, yellowish colour. The walls of veins, arteries and other blood vessels are made out of a protein called **collagen**. Like most proteins, collagen looks yellowish or white when you shape it into solid lumps.

Large arteries have thick walls to cope with the high-pressure blood being pumped straight out of the heart. So they contain lots of collagen, and appear a dull yellow or white. Veins have thinner walls than arteries, so are a little more transparent, but have a similar whitish or yellowish colour. Below a certain size, both types of blood vessel are thin enough for you to see the reddish hues of blood reflected from within. So small veins, arterioles and capillaries look bright or dark red. But once you get inside the body to look at them *none* of these blood vessels are actually blue.

But I've seen pictures of them in books. The heart is red, the lungs are purple, arteries are red and veins are blue. Right?

Sadly, no. Most biology books add a little colour to their pictures of organs and blood vessels to make them easier to understand (and, most likely, to make them look a bit more interesting and colourful). In these diagrams, they colour-code arteries and veins differently to point out their different functions. Arteries, as we know, carry oxygen-rich blood from the lungs and heart to the rest of the body. Then the oxygen gets used up in tissues and organs, and veins carry the waste-filled, deoxygenated blood back to the heart and lungs to dump carbon dioxide and get loaded up with oxygen again.

So that makes the wasted, veiny blood go blue, right?

No, it doesn't. Although the blood found in arteries is a little different in colour to that found in veins, neither of these actually contains blue blood.

Arterial blood (or the fresh, oxygen-rich blood found in arteries) appears bright red because that's the colour of light reflected by the haemoglobin proteins in red blood cells when they're bound to oxygen. But by the time it reaches your veins the oxygen in the blood has been lost – or rather, dropped off at needy cells and tissues all over the body. When the oxygen detaches from the haemoglobin protein, it changes shape and reflects less red light. So this makes **venous blood** (or the blood found in veins) more of a dark maroon colour.

But my veins *are* blue! I'm looking at one in my arm right now!

Beneath the skin some veins may *look* blue, yes. But that's not because they *are* blue, or hold blue blood. As we now know, veins are clear or yellowish and the blood in them is dark red or maroon. It's just that some veins are *at the right depth* beneath the skin to *appear* blue when white light shines on to them and bounces off again. Blood vessels right at the surface of the skin appear red, helping to give your skin its healthy, pinkish glow. Veins or arteries deeper than a millimetre beneath the skin can't be seen at all, as light won't penetrate deep enough to reach them and bounce off them.

But 'shallow' veins around half a millimetre beneath the skin can be seen. It's these vessels that appear blue, because at this depth light can shine into them, where the dark blood inside absorbs more of the red part of the light than the surrounding skin does. This makes the reflected light from these shallow veins look blue by comparison.

So if an artery was that close to the surface it would look blue too?

Right. The thin veins in your arm only *look* blue because of a trick of the light. They're just the right distance to *appear* blue beneath the skin. If a similar-sized artery was there instead, that would look bluish too. But because arteries carry higher-pressure blood, they sit deeper inside the body, where they're safer from being cut or damaged.

So blood is *always* red?

Right. Unless it clots or is left to dry out in the air. Then it goes a rusty brown colour as the red blood cells inside break down.

And never blue? Not even for royalty?

Nope. Kings, queens, princes and princesses are all red-blooded. So they're just like the rest of us.

Except the rest of us don't have crowns. Or live in castles.

Errr . . . right. Good point.

3. Food Tubes and Plop Gates

Does the colour of sick depend on what you've just eaten?
Usually, yes. Since vomit is most often simply half-digested food brought back up, its colour is usually a sloppy mix of the colourful foods you just pigged out on. But, more rarely, illness and poisoning can make your chunder go some pretty funky shades.

Sick is *usually* just a mix of foods?
Usually, yes. Your average puddle of sick, vomit, puke or chunder* is most often just a sloppy mass of saliva, mucus and half-digested food, brought back up before your stomach and intestines could finish their job. If you just ate it a few minutes ago, it will probably be the exact same colour that the food started out. This might include leafy green, a meaty or chocolatey brown or the brighter shades of food colourings from – for example – the huge box of sweets you just scarfed.

But sometimes there are other things in your vomit – besides food – that may contribute to its colour too.

---

* Choose your own favourite word here. I also like 'technicolour yawn' and 'street pizza'.

Other things? Like what?
Like bits of your stomach lining, brightly coloured digestive juices and – if you're really unlucky – blood.

Urrrrrrgh! Nasty. So why do we throw up anyway? Is it just to get rid of extra food when we eat too much?
That's one reason, yes. If you eat or drink too much, or too quickly for your digestive system to handle, nerves in your swollen stomach send a signal to a part of the brain called the **emetic centre**. This, in turn, triggers the muscles in your **oesophagus** (or food tube) to push some or all of the stomach's contents back up to your mouth. When you swallow a lump of food, muscles in the wall of your oesophagus contract in downward waves, pushing the food down the throat and into the stomach. This wave-like squeezing is called **peristalsis**, and each successful swallow is done with its own **peristaltic wave**.

To bring your sloppy sick back up, your stomach muscles contract to help squeeze its contents up into the oesophagus. From there, it's just like swallowing in reverse. Peristalsis pushes the food upwards with a series of rising waves, until the slop reaches your mouth.

Yuck! So throwing up happens for other reasons too?
Right. While the process of 'chucking up' stays more

or less the same, it can come about for lots of reasons besides overeating.

Vomiting can be a reaction to eating rotten food, toxic plants and fungi, or to drugs, alcohol and other toxic substances. If your digestive system detects these, your brain may trigger vomiting to help clear the poisons and toxins from the body.*

Another reason for vomiting is to clear the throat of trapped objects and prevent choking. This is called gagging, and it's triggered by the **gag reflex** (also called the **pharyngeal reflex**). When a swallowed object gets stuck and threatens to stop your breathing, it presses on nerves in the soft palate (in the roof of your mouth) or the back of your throat. These nerves signal the brain to trigger the peristaltic 'puke waves' we met earlier, which – along with the contents of your stomach – may help dislodge the object and clear your airways again. Interestingly, not everybody has this reflex, and people may differ in how sensitive it is. One third of people have no gag reflex at all, while others are so sensitive that they gag every time a toothbrush touches the roof of their mouth.

What about when you get ill? Being sick can make you . . . errr . . . _get_ sick too. Right?
That's true, it can. Throwing up can be a symptom of

---

* Sometimes this works and sometimes it doesn't. All these things are best avoided altogether if you don't want to throw up or be poisoned.

disease, and is often a sign of infection by viruses or bacteria. When that happens, the stomach becomes so irritated and sensitive that almost anything can make you throw up, even drinking pure water. Some microbes have evolved to trigger vomiting in this way in order to spread themselves around and infect others. So it's a clever (if somewhat gross) tactic.

Finally, vomiting can also be triggered by fear, nervousness or anxiety. This may happen as your body responds to fear by drawing blood away from your digestive system and into your muscles, preparing you to fight or run away (this is called the **adrenal** or **fight-or-flight response** – more about this later on). The effect can be anything from 'butterflies in the tummy' to queasiness to full-on puking. Which is no fun at all when you're playing the lead part in the school play.

Niiiiiice. Okay – last question. How many different colours can sick go?
Lots. As I said, it mostly depends on what you've eaten. But there are a few colours that are serious danger signs when they crop up. Bright yellow or green vomit often means you've emptied your stomach, and **bile**[*] is flowing into it from the gall bladder and intestines below. It may not be such a bad sign in itself, but if

---

[*] Bile is a neon-yellow-green digestive liquid made in your liver and stored in your gall bladder, which helps to digest fats. See page 70 for more detail on what it does in the body.

you've puked that much, you may need to **rehydrate** with water and salts to recover fully. More worrying is red, black or rusty-brown vomit. These can be signs of bleeding in the throat, oesophagus or stomach. So if you see these colours, you may want to see a doctor, sharpish.

What about bright blue or purple sick?
That just means you've been eating the crayons again. So stop it.

Oh. Oops!

Why does bad food give you diarrhoea?

Because it's filled with nasty microbes that affect your guts, making the lining swell up and preventing it from absorbing water from your poo. The result is what's medically known as diarrhoea and more commonly known as the runs or the trots.

Urrrrrrrrr! The runs? That is *nasty*!
It certainly is. And, while it is kind of fun to joke about it sometimes, severe diarrhoea is no laughing matter. If your body is poisoned or infected by dangerous microbes in your food, it's actually possible to suffer diarrhoea so severe that it can kill you. You literally poo yourself to death.

Okay – that's just about the worst thing I can imagine. So what are microbes, and how do they get in your food?
Microbes are micro-organisms – including viruses, bacteria and other microscopic life-forms – which live everywhere on Earth, and inside the bodies of every animal on the planet. Whenever you eat a piece of food – whether it's meat, fruit or vegetable – you're also eating the microbes that live inside it. It's these microbes, and the toxic chemicals they create, that cause diarrhoea once they get inside you.

Yuck! But if that were true, then wouldn't they give you the runs every time you ate something?
Ahh, but here's the clever bit. Your body filters the food you eat as it passes through your digestive system. After your food is mashed up and dissolved in acids and digestive juices, the whole sloppy lot passes through your intestines, where most of this filtering is done.

There, special cells lining the spongy, knobbly gut wall pump water and nutrients out of the sloppy food and into the bloodstream. But these same cells also form a sieve-like barrier to microbes inside the food, leaving them trapped inside the gut. By the time your food arrives at the rectum – the exit tunnel of your intestines – most of the nutrients and water have been extracted, leaving dried-up lumps of bacteria and undigested food. Otherwise known as faeces.

. . . or good, honest poo.
Exactly.

So if everything works as it's supposed to, the nasties are prevented from entering your body by your gut cells, become trapped inside your poo, and are removed every time you drop a 'number two'. And even if a few bacteria *do* manage to squidge through the barrier, they usually don't make it far. In the cell layers just behind it, they quickly encounter antibodies and immune cells that surround and destroy them before they can make it into the bloodstream and do

ANTIBODY V BACTERIA

more damage.
Unless, that is, you eat bad food, laden with especially toxic bacteria. Microbes like this grow inside all types of food, and any food will be teeming with them if left for long enough. But they're found in greater numbers (and grow especially quickly) inside beef, pork and chicken, which is why we usually cook meat and fish to kill off the bugs inside before we eat it.* It is possible to eat raw meat if it's very, very fresh, but it doesn't take long before the bacteria begin to multiply and the meat 'goes bad'.

Unless you stick it in the fridge. Then it keeps a bit longer, right?
Right. Keeping food cool in the fridge slows down the growth of bacteria.** But eventually they'll grow, spread and break down proteins, fats and sugars inside the food. As this happens, the food changes colour and the bacteria release sour-smelling waste

---

* Either that or we smoke or salt (cure) them – both of which will help kill off the nasty bacteria too.

** And freezing stops them growing altogether, which is why frozen food can keep for months.

products (which is why 'off' or 'bad' food goes brown and smells funny). Eat a rotten piece of meat, fruit or veg in this state, and your guts are in for some serious trouble.

As the 'bad' food arrives at your intestines, your body does its best to keep the nasties out. But there are now so many that your guts become a battleground. On the one side, an army of nasty, aggressive microbes are trying to squeeze their way through the gut lining. On the other, the cells of your body's defence (or immune) system try to hold the line, and call for reinforcements from the bloodstream. In the process, your gut lining swells up, allowing cells from the bloodstream to enter the gut tissues and join the battle. And while this does help stop bacteria from passing the spongy barrier of the gut wall, it also prevents water and nutrients from passing. Which is bad news for your body.

Why's that?
Because, as we've already learned, your body likes to absorb water and nutrients from the pre-digested food slopping through your intestines. If it can't do this, then not only will your poo remain sloppy, but your body will also be unable to get the water, minerals and nutrients it needs to keep functioning.

That doesn't sound too good.
It isn't. The first effect of all this is diarrhoea, as the

poo arrives at the muscle (called the anal sphincter) guarding the exit to your rectum in a liquid state, and in something of a hurry. Ordinarily, chunks of nicely dried-out faeces would arrive at the rectum and pile up there – held in check by the gatekeeping sphincter muscle until you're ready to visit the loo. But when the poo arrives as a liquid, the sphincter gets confused, and often mistakes it for a harmless cloud of gut gases.

All too late, the sphincter realizes its mistake, and you're left with the difficult task of sprinting for the loo with your buttocks squeezed tightly together. If you're lucky, you'll make it in time. If not, well . . .

So what happens then?
The diarrhoea continues as the battle in your gut rages on. But your body usually prevails over the bugs, and eventually everything in your gut returns to normal. You might need to drink some fluids and salts to replace those you've lost, but otherwise you'll be fine.

But if the battle (and the diarrhoea) continues for more than a few days, your body can become weak and malnourished, so you may need to visit the doctor and get antibiotics or other medicines to help your body win the battle. But, again, after a little rest and recovery you'll be fine.

So I'm not likely to poo myself to death, then?
No. Not likely. With the help of today's medicines,

deaths from food poisoning are very rare. And while it *is* possible to poo yourself to death, diarrhoea this severe only usually comes with serious water-borne diseases like cholera and typhoid, rather than from eating bad food.

Phew! That's a relief.
What do you mean?

Well, I ate a dodgy week-old sausage I found in the fridge yesterday, and something's definitely going on downstairs today. Feels kind of gurgly, and . . . uh-oh!

Why are some farts eggier than others?

Because diets and digestive systems vary. A fart is just a mixture of gases that builds up in your intestines and trumps its way out of your bottom. It's the foods you eat and your ability to digest them that affect which gases are in that mixture. Which, in turn, determines the 'egg factor' of each 'bottom burp'.

There's an actual 'egg factor' that scientists use to measure farts? Brilliant!

Well . . . no. Not officially. But if there was you could predict where on the scale each fart (or flatus) would fall, based on what the farter had eaten over the last few days. It comes down to diet, and how much of your food remains undigested by the time it hits your large intestine.

Is that where farts are made?

Sort of, yes. Farts actually contain a mixture of gases from a few different sources. There's oxygen and nitrogen from the air you swallow with your food. There's carbon dioxide from swallowed air, fizzy drinks and fizzing stomach acids. And then there's more carbon dioxide – plus hydrogen, hydrogen sulphide and methane – produced by bacteria in the lower intestine.

Wow. That sounds like a lot of gas. How much fart gas do we actually make?

As it happens, quite a bit. The average healthy person creates a daily 1–2.5 litres (2–4 pints) of gas, and releases it – in the shape of individual farts – about twelve to sixteen times a day.

Sixteen farts a day is *normal*?

Yep. Unless they're particularly loud or stinky, most people don't even realize they're dropping them. And – whatever they may try to tell you – girls fart just as often as boys. (It's just that they're far less likely to award themselves a mark out of ten, and wait for a round of applause.) Someone with a *real* fart (or flatulence) problem will fart upwards of fifty times a day. And when they drop one you'll *know* it.

So what exactly is it that makes a fart stinky?

In short, the ingredients you're 'cooking' it with. Of all the gases in the fart mix we mentioned earlier, most don't really smell at all. Nitrogen, oxygen, hydrogen, carbon dioxide and methane are all completely odourless gases. So it's usually the hydrogen sulphide that's the culprit. Ask your chemistry teacher to give you a quick whiff of a jar of hydrogen sulphide and you'll see what I mean. The eggy pong will almost knock your head off.

Hydrogen sulphide is generally released into the fart mix by bacteria in your large intestine. These bacteria helpfully and happily munch away at anything that you're not able to digest fully, releasing methane, carbon dioxide and hydrogen sulphide gas in the process. The amount of stinky gas they produce depends on the amount and type of undigested food that arrives in your intestines. Which, in turn, depends on what you eat, and how good you are at digesting it before it reaches the 'fart bugs'.

Go on, then – which are the best foods for maximum fartiness?

Well, if you really *wanted* to cook up a gutful of stinky air-biscuits, you'd want to eat foods with lots of complex sugars, starches and fibre. (These are difficult to digest, and pretty much ensure the fart bugs have something to work with.)

These 'fart foods' include beans, peas, onions, cabbage, broccoli, sprouts, wheat, prunes and pasta. Contrary to popular belief, fatty meats and sausages don't really cause farts, nor make them particularly eggy.* So if you want to load up on fart ingredients before unleashing your bottom on the whole class at school, you're better off sticking with the veggies.

I must warn you, though – this may be hilarious to the boys but is unlikely to make you popular with the

---

* Although they may vary the aroma in other ways. When I was a university student, my friend and roommate once woke me up in the middle of the night to 'appreciate' the fart he had just done, which he said smelled exactly like the roast chicken he'd eaten for dinner. Fortunately, I had a cold and couldn't smell a thing.

girls. Or, for that matter, your teacher.

All right, all right. So what should I do if I want to *avoid* having eggy farts?
For starters, try to eat and drink more slowly, so that you swallow less air and produce less gas by volume. Then limit the amount of starchy, hard-to-digest food you eat. Try to balance out your intake of pasta, wheat, meat and vegetables. And, in particular, ease up on the baked beans and cabbage.

One more thing to try would be to get tested for lactose intolerance. Lactose is a sugar found in dairy products, which a number of people (especially those with African or Asian origins) are unable to digest properly, leading to more farts than usual. So, if it turns out you do have lactose intolerance, then the best way to avoid the 'eggers' may be to decrease your intake of milk, cheese and other dairy products.

In other words, I should 'cut the cheese'?
Oh, very funny.

Mwahahahahahaaa!

GET IT SORTED: FACTS ABOUT FARTS

- Baked beans really do make you fart. They contain a sugar called stachoise which is hard for human guts to break down. So bacteria try to do it for us, producing a lot of gas in the process. So beans really *are* the 'musical fruit'. (The more you eat, the more you toot . . .)

- If you farted while floating in Space (assuming the fart could escape your suit) the physical reaction would propel you in the opposite direction. Just like a rocket, only slower.

- Chris Warren of Manchester, England, holds the world record for 'longest medley of farts'. In February 2003, he did fourteen farts in a row, with no more than two seconds between each.

If fatty foods make you fat, do sugary foods make you sweet?

Not really, no. In fact, it's sugary foods – not fatty ones – that make most people overweight. And while eating too much fat isn't healthy we do need some fat in our diets to keep our bodies in good condition.

Hold on – what? You mean I need to be fat to be healthy?

Not 'be fat', no. Being overweight can cause all sorts of other problems in your body. But if you want to stay healthy then you do need to *eat* fat. You need *all three* of the major food types – fat, protein and carbohydrates – to build and protect all the tissues of a strong, healthy body. It's just a case of getting the right stuff in the right amounts. In the end, you are – quite literally – what you eat.

Exactly. So if you *eat* fat, you *are* fat, right?

Well, it's not quite as simple as that, I'm afraid.

Why?

Because, for starters, most foods contain at least two of the three food groups. Most vegetables, for example, contain both proteins and carbohydrates, while meat and fish contain protein, fat *and* carbohydrates. Plus, all these food types are processed in complex ways. When you swallow a lump of meaty protein, it isn't just sucked immediately into a muscle. It's digested, broken down, passed into your bloodstream and may be used as an energy source or building block within any one of your body's tissues. And the same goes for fats and carbohydrates.

Huh?

Okay – here's how it all works.

We get our **fats** (or **lipids**) mostly from fatty meat, milk, cheese, butter, nuts and vegetable oils. Inside the body, fats are broken into smaller blobs by bile salts. These are stored and released by an organ called the **gall bladder**, which sits just beneath the liver. From there, the fat globs pass to the small intestine, where special enzymes* called **lipases** break them down into small **fatty acids**. These are then absorbed and either used for energy, used to build the membranes around cells or stored in fat (or **adipose**) cells.

Proteins, too, are mostly scoffed in the form of meat, milk and cheese, along with beans, nuts, fish, eggs and vegetables. Once inside the body, special enzymes called **proteases** – released by the stomach, pancreas and small intestine – break proteins down into **amino acids**. These are then used for energy, to build new body tissues, to build antibodies for the

---

* An **enzyme** is a type of protein that breaks down or joins together other molecules. Enzymes in washing powder break down oily stains on your clothes. Enzymes in your body do all sorts of clever things, including breaking down food, building muscle tissue, destroying bacteria and copying DNA.

immune system or for any number of other clever purposes in the body. Any leftover amino acids are converted into a chemical called **urea** (meaning 'urine stuff') in the liver. Which is then – you guessed it – passed to the kidneys and out of the body as **urine**.

Carbohydrates include simple **sugars** like **glucose** and **fructose**, and also complex **starches** (which are like long, tough chains of sugars, all linked together). So perhaps not surprisingly we get them mostly from sweet, sugary foods like chocolate, and from starchy foods like bread, rice, potatoes and pasta. Carbohydrates are broken down by enzymes released by salivary glands, the pancreas and the small intestine. In the end, most of what's left is simple glucose. Once absorbed into the bloodstream, glucose is either used immediately for energy, used to build fibrous tissues, stored in muscles, or converted to fatty acids and stored in fat cells.

Okay, I get all that. I think.
Good.

But if both fats and sugars are stored in fat cells, then don't *both* of them make you fat?
In short, yes. But in reality it's usually the sugars (or, rather, the carbohydrates) that do it. This happens for two reasons:

1) Fat makes you feel full when you eat it, which generally prevents you from eating too much. That's

why you can easily polish off a massive bowl of pasta, but getting through a similar-sized bowl filled with beefburgers would be much harder work.

2) Fat can be expensive. Steaks, chicken legs, pork chops, rich cheeses and exotic nuts are all very costly compared with bread, rice, white pasta and potatoes. Which is why most of us fill up on carbohydrates, with just a small portion of meat on top, on the side, or in between.

But that's a good thing, isn't it?

Yes, that's fine. As long as you eat the right kinds of carbohydrates, and not too much of the wrong ones. Beans, vegetables, brown rice and brown bread are good, because they contain complex carbohydrates that make you feel full and take a long time to digest, making you feel fuller for longer. But sugar, sweets, chocolate, white rice, white bread and white pasta all break down very quickly in the body, leaving you feeling hungry again soon after eating them. Because of this, you're more likely to eat too much of them, and more of the sugars released in digestion will be stored as fat.

And, perhaps worst of all, too many sugary foods can mess up your body's ability to control the level of sugar in your blood. So they not only make you fatter and hungrier, they also increase your risk of developing other problems like diabetes, high blood pressure and heart disease.

Wow. That doesn't sound too 'sweet'. So what's the right amount to eat?

It depends on your age, your body type and the way your body processes food. But one good way of balancing your foods is to split your dinner plate into quarters (not literally – your mum won't thank you for that). Then you fill the first quarter with foods rich in fat and protein, like meat, fish or beans. The second quarter, you load with carbohydrates like rice, pasta or potatoes. Then the remaining half, you fill with vegetables like green beans or salad greens. Stick to that, and you can't go too far wrong.

Wait a minute – where does the ice cream and chocolate come into all this?

After dinner, not instead of it. Eat a good, balanced diet, and you can happily enjoy a scoop of ice cream or a few chunks of chocolate each day.

Phew! That's a relief. Okay, so let's talk about these scoops . . . Am I allowed to use a shovel?

[Sigh] I give up.

Puzzle: diet and digestion wordsearch

Have you digested all these gut-related words? Find as many as you can in the grid below. (Double your score if you can remember what they all mean!) Answers on page 234.

amino acids	carbohydrates	fats	fatty acids
gall bladder	intestine	lipases	lipids
liver	oesophagus	peristalsis	proteases
proteins	starches	stomach	sugars

```
I S D Y P E R I S T A L S I S E C X S G C L
B U K H S T O X K V O V I N T E S T I N E C
F G A V I A V U R M E U N V S O Q Y R R W Q
M A C X Q G A L L B L A D D E R G Z K W Y E
P H J L P S V T Z R M P T S K R S A T X G L
H P P G A K T A L I P I D S T U E N I G O L
P O S I O G Y A N M X L F U I A S O D A H T
Y S G Z H N S O F P I F A T T Y A C I D S Z
Y E U W B C A R B O H Y D R A T E S N M A S
X O N G P C R V D M D G X P R O T E I N S Q
H G R L I P A S E S T O M A C H O W P S D S
U M R D X J U X K Z R J G D D P R K Y X Y T
H L S U G A R S E H C R A T S H P J F D R Q
L B E M U J I D N U D Z S N A W C J P S N T
```

74

How long could you survive without food or water?

In general, not long. A good rough guide is 'three days without water, six weeks without food'. But while some have survived starvation for months on end, others have died of dehydration in a matter of hours. It all depends on your health, fitness, body fat, body temperature and how your body processes food.

You can die of thirst in a couple of hours?
In the right (or rather the wrong) conditions, yes. If you got extremely hot – and you were ill, unfit or unhealthy – then a few hours without water could be enough to kill you.

Wow. Why does your body need water so much more than food? Doesn't food give us the energy we need to live?
Yes, it does. But while food provides us with energy, we can't make use of that energy without enough water in our bodies. Water does many, many essential things in the body. Without it, we can't get at the energy inside the food we eat, nor get that energy to where it's needed. Without water, we can't eat, we can't move and our cells gradually collapse and die.

Oh. So it's pretty important, then.
I'd say so, yes. Your body is mostly made of water.

Between 55 and 60 per cent, to be exact. Your bones are 10–15 per cent water. Your brain is about 85 per cent water. Water fills almost every cell in your body and most of the spaces in between them. Oxygen and nutrients must travel through the watery bloodstream to reach the brain, the heart and all the essential life-giving organs of the body. Carbon dioxide and other wastes must travel the same watery pathways to your lungs, liver and kidneys for removal. Water is the key ingredient of all living organisms. And, as far as we know, life itself is impossible without it.

Now think about this – every minute of every day, you're losing water to your environment through breathing, sweating, pooing and peeing.* If you don't replace that water quickly enough, the result is **dehydration**.

Denied the water it so desperately needs, your body tries to save all it can. You stop sweating. You stop peeing. Your mouth becomes dry. Your eyeballs dry out and get sucked into their sockets as water drains from them and into the bloodstream. Your heart beats faster, trying to spread what little water is left to the thirsty tissues all over your body. But eventually it fails.

In the end your blood pressure drops, your skin goes cold and your brain shuts down for good.

---

* Well, you don't poo and pee every *minute*, naturally. But with each passing minute, more and more water piles up in your bladder and intestines – destined to be lost with the next trip to the loo.

Yikes. Scary. So how long would all that take?
On average, about three to five days. If you're very fit and healthy, maybe a day or two more. But if you're ill, unfit, sweltering in a heatwave, lost in a desert or trapped in a car or greenhouse, then dehydration can begin in hours and be all over within a day.

Why does being ill or unfit make a difference?
Because if you're ill it takes extra energy and water to maintain your body, and many illnesses (like cholera) also cause diarrhoea and vomiting, which make you lose water faster. Even if you're not actually *ill*, being unfit makes a difference too. Your level of fitness affects your **metabolism**, or the rate at which your body uses up its water and energy reserves. And it usually also determines how much body fat you have and how well you can control your body temperature. These things make a *big* difference to your ability to survive dehydration.

They also affect your ability to survive a long-term lack of food – otherwise known as **starvation**. It takes the average person around forty days (or six weeks) to starve to death.* But, depending on your body condition, you might die without food in little over two weeks, or survive for three months or more.

---

* If you're interested, the average for dogs is thirty-eight days – although some can go as long as 117 days without food! For cats, it's twenty days. For guinea pigs, eight days, and for mice, rats and gerbils just two to three days.

So who would last longer without food – a fat guy, or a skinny guy?
What do you think?

I reckon the fat bloke. He could live off his extra flab for ages before he even started starving, right?
Well, unfortunately (for the fat bloke, at least) starvation doesn't quite work like that. After just one day without food, your body enters the first stage of starvation, and begins to use up the sugars in your tissues and bloodstream. Within two to three days, your body realizes it's still not getting any food, and kicks into phase two of emergency starvation mode. Since your brain's preferred energy source is sugar (or, more specifically, glucose), it starts saving some of its remaining sugar reserves, and starts eating into your fat instead. In this stage, it breaks down fat into fatty acids. Which, at a push, your brain will put up with using as an energy source instead of glucose.

There you go, you see? The fat bloke could survive like that for ages . . .
Ah, but that's not the whole story. While fat is a high-energy food source, it's also very stable and hard to break down. (Think how long it takes to burn a candle versus melting a spoonful of sugar.) So, even if you have plenty of fat reserves, your body can't break them down fast enough to supply all the energy your

brain needs. So it has to eat into your body's **protein** stores too.

For the first few days it just nibbles away at your skeletal muscle, thinning out your arms and legs a bit. But after *several* days of starvation your body goes into phase three, and starts eating into protein from all the cells, tissues and organs of your body – including the liver, the kidneys and the heart. At this point it really doesn't matter how much fat you have left. Your brain, desperate to save itself, ignores the slow-burning fat and continues eating into the quick-burning, energy-rich proteins of your body instead. Within forty days (on average), so much protein has been eaten away that your organs begin to fail, one by one. Eventually the heart muscle becomes too weak to keep pumping, and starvation ends abruptly with a **cardiac arrest**, or heart attack.

But wouldn't someone with more fat survive for a bit longer in phase two?

Sadly, no. Unless the skinny bloke was *very* skinny or starving to begin with, the fat bloke's extra fat would make little difference. It *might* help him survive if he was lost without food in the Arctic, where the added insulation of his fat layers would mean he'd use less energy keeping warm than the skinny guy. Then again, if he was lost and starving in a hot desert, the extra fat might speed up the fat bloke's demise, as he would use more energy trying to stay cool (and probably die of heatstroke or dehydration long before he starved).

This is one of the reasons why people native to colder regions (like the Inuit tribes of Canada and Alaska) generally have a heavier build than the original tribes of Africa, Australia and Indonesia. Hunters everywhere go through times of plenty and times when food is scarce. But while having more body fat really helps when you're hungry and cold, it's no help at all if you're hungry and hot.

Hmmm. This whole thing's making me hungry right now.
What? When did you last eat?

About an hour ago. Yeah, yeah – I know that I *could* survive several weeks without a chocolate biscuit, but that doesn't mean I actually *want* to . . .

If you stopped peeing for a month, would you explode?

No, you wouldn't. Unless your pee tubes were blocked, you wouldn't make it anywhere near that long. Long before your bladder became filled to bursting point, the muscle that holds your pee tube shut would give out. So you wouldn't explode – you'd just pee your pants (and be very embarrassed).

Seriously? I have a pee muscle in my pee tube?
More like around your pee tube. But, yes, you do. Just as a circular sphincter muscle prevents poo from falling out of your gut, another sphincter muscle holds your pee tube (or **urethra**) closed, and stops your from leaking into your pants all day long. One reason why peeing feels like such a *relief* is that you're letting go of (or relaxing) this muscle to do it. You don't really need to push or squeeze – your stretchy bladder just deflates and empties like a balloon, and the urine flows out freely until the pressure drops and the sphincter muscle tightens up again.

Hmmm. Never really thought about it like that. So the bladder is where your pee comes from?
The bladder is where your pee (or urine) is stored, but it's not where your urine is made.

So where does that happen? In the stomach?

Not quite, no. Many people seem to have the idea that the solid foods you eat and the liquids you drink follow different paths through the body – that hamburgers and chips travel through the stomach and gut to become poo, while orange juice and cola travel some other path to become urine in the bladder. But this isn't really how it works at all.

Everything you eat and drink flows into your digestive system (namely, your stomach and guts). There, the whole lot mixes together into a messy sludge, and nutrients and water are drawn out into the bloodstream. The undigested stuff left in your digestive system then exits your body as faeces (i.e. poo). This is called **excretion**. But that's not the only way your body gets rid of wastes. The other major way is through **urine**. This is made in your **urinary system**, by filtering excess water and wastes from your blood.

So urine isn't undigested water, cola and orange juice – it's actually what's filtered out from blood?
Exactly.

So where are the blood filters in your body?
In your kidneys. These are the most important parts of your urinary system. Usually, you have two kidneys*,

---

* Although you don't necessarily need two of them to live. Some people are born with one, and do just fine. Others even volunteer to *donate* one of their kidneys to people who need a new one. In both cases, the remaining kidney grows by up to 50 per cent, and happily takes up the work of the missing one.

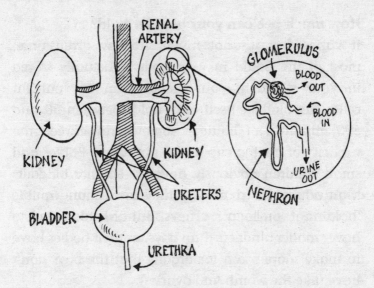

and each one receives blood from a large **renal artery**. Inside the kidney, these branch into smaller and smaller blood vessels, eventually ending in a tiny, ball-shaped knot of capillaries called a **glomerulus**. From there, water and wastes move through special filtering membranes into a kind of watery-waste-collecting tube called a **nephron**. There are about 1.25 million of these per kidney, and each nephron flows into a collecting duct. Eventually, these ducts all join together and funnel the salty, waste-filled urine (made from freshly-filtered blood) to a big exit tube in the centre of the kidney, called a **ureter**. The two ureters (one from each kidney) then carry urine down to the bladder, where it is stored until you're ready to pee, or until the bladder is full – whichever comes first.

How much pee can your bladder hold?

It varies, but it's not much. At any given time, most of the liquid in your body is actually stored in your stomach, your bloodstream or your fat cells. The bladder itself only holds between 50 and 500 millilitres of liquid – somewhere between the capacity of an egg cup and a pint glass. Babies and small children obviously have far smaller bladders than adults, which is why they have more trouble 'holding it' on long journeys. But girls also tend to have smaller bladders than boys, as their bodies have to make more room for organs that the boys don't have (like the womb and ovaries).

However large or small it is, once the bladder becomes full, it swells and stretches, and nerves around your bladder send signals to the brain, giving you the urge to pee. Urine moves down the urethra until it meets the urethral sphincter muscle, which allows you to keep this 'exit tube' closed while you 'hold it'. Once you've found a loo (or a secluded spot in the woods), you simply let go of this muscle, and the urine rushes out of your urethra to the outside. If you go straight away, it just flows out with a gentle tinkle. If you've been holding it for a while, then more pressure builds up in the bladder, and it empties itself with a more impressive, gushing stream.

So how long can you hold it in, once you've felt the urge?

Again, that varies. It depends on what you've been drinking, how much and how fast you've been drinking it, and on the size of your bladder. It can be anywhere from thirty minutes to several days. But, in general, once you've felt the urge, you should go as soon as possible.

Why? Could you actually explode?
No, you won't explode. Once your bladder fills and stretches beyond a certain point, you immediately lose control your urethral sphincter muscle, and your bladder spontaneously empties itself – regardless of whether you're on the loo, sitting in class or riding a bike. So, unless your urinary system is damaged or blocked, you could never build up enough pressure to explode.

That said, trying to 'hold it' for long periods of time isn't good for you either. While you might not explode, stretching your urinary system like this can damage the soft tissues of your urethra, your bladder or even your kidneys, leading to painful infections and other problems.

Ouch! Okay – I guess next time I need to go . . .
I'll just *go*.
Right. Believe me, no three-hour movie or game-a-thon is worth an embarrassing puddle and a painful pee tube . . .

Why do teeth fall out, and why don't they grow back in grown-ups?

Baby (or 'milk') teeth are temporary chompers that fall out to make room for bigger, stronger adult teeth later on. Adult teeth fall out when they become damaged, decayed and infected by bacteria. Once this second set of teeth has grown in, you're done. When they're gone, they're gone. This is because nature figures you're set for life, and the gene that controls regrowth of your gnashers switches off.

Hang on a mo – why do we even have milk teeth? Why don't we just grow one set and keep 'em?
Because the wide, strong set of teeth you need as an adult would be too big for your head (or rather, your jaw) as a baby. That said, you still need *some* kind of chompers to get you through your first years of life. So milk teeth (or, as dentists call them, **deciduous teeth**)* are tiny, temporary 'pegs' that do the job while your jawbones are still growing.

What job? It's not as if you need a full set of teeth to eat baby food. It's all mashed up already!
Ah, but that's because someone else has done the mashing already. It the modern, developed world,

---

* *Deciduous* comes from the Latin for 'to fall off or fall out'. The same word is used elsewhere in biology, too. *Deciduous* trees are trees with leaves or needles that fall off every year, like maples, willows and birch trees.

machines in baby-food factories mash up baby food during the production process. Elsewhere – and throughout history, before we had machines – parents would pre-mash or pre-chew solid food for their babies before giving it to them. But, either way, someone (or something) has to do the mashing.

Because, basically, that's what teeth are for. They mash up solid food into small, soft lumps that can be swallowed and digested without damaging – or getting stuck in – your digestive system. As you may already know, you have three main types of teeth in your jaw – incisors, canines and molars.

Incisors are blade-like shearing teeth, which help slice into your food. **Canines** are grabbing and tearing teeth, used for ripping chunks of meat off the bone. **Molars** (and their smaller cousins, the **premolars**) are chewing teeth. They're used for grinding nuts and seeds, breaking up tough, chewy plant and animal tissues, and mashing each mouthful of food into a soft pulp. As you might expect, plant-eating **herbivores** like cows lack sharp canines, while meat-eating **carnivores** have pointy molars more suited to slicing than grinding. Humans, chimps and other **omnivores** have both kinds, since we need them to munch both meat *and* veggies.

So how many teeth do we have?
A normal adult human has thirty-two teeth – sixteen in the upper jaw and sixteen in the lower jaw. (To

locate them all for yourself, see the **DIY Dentistry** box on page 91.) But they don't all grow through at once. For the first set of milk teeth, the incisors grow first, when you're between five and eight months old. Then come the canines and molars (which start arriving from one year onwards). By the time you're two and a half, all your deciduous teeth are through. Then around six to eight years of age, your jaw has grown large enough for your permanent adult teeth to come through. So the milk teeth begin falling out, and the whole cycle of growth repeats itself. First the incisors are replaced (leaving many six to eight-year-olds with gappy grins for a bit), then the canines, premolars and molars. By the time you're twelve or thirteen, all but your third set of molars (the wisdom teeth) will be present. (These may or may not come through later on, usually around eighteen to twenty-one years, but sometimes much later and sometimes not at all.)

After that, you're done. Then it's just a case of looking after your permanent teeth for life – protecting them from damage, decay and disease. If one of these teeth gets knocked out by a hockey stick, or eaten down to the root by bacteria, then chances are* it won't grow back again. Ever.

---

* There have been rare cases of elderly people growing lost adult teeth back, but these are very rare exceptions and you definitely shouldn't expect it to happen.

But why not? Why can't damaged teeth repair themselves, or grow back again after they fall out? As a matter of fact, your teeth *are* repairing themselves all the time. Just as bones grow continually (but slowly) and reshape themselves throughout life, so do your teeth. Teeth grow from the soft root and pulp below into the hard outer dentine and enamel layers above. As the surface of a tooth is worn down from use, it is slowly replaced by new tissue from within.

But if bacteria are allowed to grow on your teeth, and eat down through the enamel and dentine into the pulp and root, then the tooth can't repair itself quickly enough. So the body seals off the root of the damaged tooth to protect itself from further infection. (A similar thing happens if the tooth is deeply cracked or knocked out in an accident – the body seals off the root to limit the damage and prevent the entry of bacteria.) With no more blood supply, the tooth will rot and die. So it either falls out by itself, or (more often) it has to be extracted by a dentist.

This is why it's so important to brush, floss and rinse your teeth every day. This prevents the bacteria from building up and eating rapidly into your teeth. And since bacteria love feeding on sugar, it's especially important to clean your teeth after sugary snacks. Looked after properly, your teeth can last an entire lifetime. But more often diet, decay, damage and accidents mean that most people end up losing some or all of their teeth by the time they reach sixty or seventy.

So then you have to get false ones, right?
Usually, yes. Once you reach adulthood, the gene that controls the natural regrowth of lost teeth gets switched off, so any lost adult teeth must be replaced with artificial teeth made of a hard plastic. Whole teeth are often attached to existing teeth using metal bridges, but they can also be screwed right into the jaw. If you lose all your teeth, you may need dentures – which are basically a full set of upper and lower acrylic teeth, complete with moulded plastic gums that slip over your own. They're usually held in place by sticky gels or adhesives, to stop them dropping out into your dinner.

Urrrgh! Yuck! I hope that never happens to me.
Well, it may never do so. Recently, scientists have been working on ultrasound implants that help stimulate teeth to repair themselves, and on special gene-therapy gels that may one day allow you to regrow lost teeth altogether!

Cool!
But . . . they're not quite ready to roll yet, and even when they are, they will probably be very expensive. So the smart thing to do is . . .

I know, I know – look after the chompers you've already got.
Exactly. So if you want to dodge the dentures, you'd better keep brushing!

DIY dentistry: check your own teeth!

Adult humans have thirty-two permanent teeth. Depending on your age, you may or may not have them all just now – some might not have grown through yet, and may be temporarily missing. But see how many you can find. Grab a hand mirror, open wide and follow these instructions to ID your teeth, just like your dentist does!

- First, the incisors. These are the two flat, horsey-looking teeth at the front, along with the two smaller teeth on either side. You should have eight altogether – four upper incisors, and four lower incisors.

- Behind those are the more pointy-looking canines. These may be quite pointy, or rounded at the bottom. Either way, they usually stick out a little compared to the teeth in front and

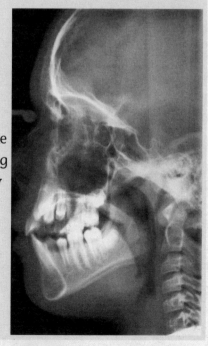

behind. You should have a total of four canines – two upper, two lower.

- Behind those are the flatter, squarer premolars. You should have eight of these – two on each side of the mouth, behind the canines, in both the upper and lower jaw.
- Finally, we come to the molars. These are large, square, flat-bottomed teeth right at the back. By your teens, there should be at least two on each side of the mouth in both the upper and lower jaw, giving a total of eight molars. After that, most (but not all) people grow a third set of four molars – known as wisdom teeth – that sit behind the original eight.
- eight incisors + four canines + eight premolars + twelve molars = thirty teeth altogether. How many did you find?

Why does your tummy rumble when you're hungry?

Because when your brain senses that you're hungry it empties your stomach, squeezing out stomach gases and half-digested slop to make room for the lovely grub to come. As these gases and liquids gurgle through your guts, they create loud rumbling noises in your belly.

Really? Like gurgling drainpipes inside your body?

Exactly. Only the pipes are meaty, and have more twists and turns. And they're filled with half-digested, liquid food (or **chyme**) rather than rainwater.

Hmmm. It doesn't sound much like a gurgle in *my* belly. More like a growling bear or something.

That's because the sound changes as it vibrates through the muscle, meaty fibres and skin of your belly, so that by the time it gets to the outside, the sound is much lower-pitched. Technically, tummy rumbles are called **borborgymi**.* And you're right – by the time they get to the outside, they sound more like low growls than tinkly gurgles. But, if you put your ear to someone's belly just as it rumbles,** you'll

---

* And if you say 'borborgymi' in a silly, low-pitched voice, it sounds like just like the thing it describes!

** Make sure you ask permission – or at least warn the person – before you do this. Otherwise you'll get some very strange looks.

hear the high gurgly bit beneath the rumble, which you can't normally hear from a distance.

But why would you want your stomach to squeeze shut if you're about to eat something? Wouldn't you want it to stay open, so you can digest things?

It doesn't really squeeze shut, it just contracts a bit to push out the stuff that's still in there, in order to make room for more. And, in fact, not much digestion goes on in the stomach at all.

Eh? I thought the stomach had acids in it that melt and digest your food for you . . .

Well, it does contain acids that break the food down a bit. And, together with the churning, mashing muscles of the stomach wall, these help liquefy your food. This is partly to make digestion easier later on, but mostly so you can fit more grub in your stomach at once. The main function of the stomach is to receive mashed-up food blobs from the mouth and hold them in storage for a bit, before they're passed through the gut for digestion.

The stomach doesn't really extract the nutrients from your food – that's the job of the intestines. Instead, the stomach is basically a big holding bag in your digestive system that allows you to eat big wedges of food at once, instead of slowly grazing and nibbling away all day. It evolved because it helps us (and other animals) to 'eat and run', snarfing large quantities of food on the move and keeping them in store for slow digestion later on.

Okay . . . so how does your brain know you're hungry in the first place?

Basically, it senses changes in the levels of sugars and fats in your bloodstream. When levels drop too low, the brain releases clever chemical messengers (called hormones) into your blood that make you feel hungry, and want to seek out food. Then when you finally find food it sends quicker signals (through nerves) to your mouth, stomach and gut, preparing them for fast and efficient grub intake. Often, even *looking* at food can be enough to trigger these nerve signals.

Is that why we sometimes drool and slobber when we see tasty-looking foods?

Yep – spot on. These brain-body (or **psychosomatic**) signals were discovered by a famous Russian biologist and psychologist named Ivan Pavlov. He revealed them by ringing a bell every time he fed a group of dogs. After a while, the dogs would drool at the sound of the bell alone, proving that it wasn't the food itself that was making the dogs slobber – it was the thought of food (or, rather, hearing something that made them think of food, even if the food wasn't present).

In the same way, when you haven't eaten for a while, and you're suddenly presented with a steak, cake or milkshake, you'll start to drool from salivary glands under your tongue and at the back of your mouth. As you munch and chew, the saliva starts to break down starchy bits of your food, and keeps it moist so that it slides down your food tube (or oesophagus) more easily.

Wow. I'm getting hungry just thinking about it.
If you like, you can go even further, and do a little brain-body experiment. Try this:

- Imagine you're lost in a hot, dry desert, and you haven't eaten for days.
- Now picture in your mind, a huge, fat, juicy hamburger. Really see it in your mind's eye, every detail – the rich, juicy meat . . . the crunchy lettuce beneath . . . the wet, juicy tomato on top . . .
- Now imagine raising the burger to your open mouth . . . the smell of it wafting up your nostrils as you take a big, juicy bite . . .
- Drooling yet?

Ohhhhhhhhhhhhhhh. Not fair. That does it – I'm off for a burger . . .
Have fun!

4. Zits, Rashes and Fightin' Bugs

If my appendix is useless, then what's it doing there?

Actually, your appendix isn't useless. For many years, it was thought to be little more than the shrivelled remains of some ancient digestive organ. This it may well be. But scientists have recently discovered that it's also a fleshy nursery for 'good' gut bacteria. So you're better off with an appendix than without.

But my textbook says that the appendix is useless. It's a vestibule organ or something.

You mean 'vestigial organ'?

Yeah, that's the one.

That's right. Many biology textbooks say that the appendix is **vestigial**, meaning that it may once have been a mighty digestive organ, but now it has all but disappeared, so serves no purpose in the human body. Another example of this is a vestigial tail. All human embryos have tails for a few weeks – a hangover from our evolutionary past, when our lemur-like ancestors grew full-on tails for curling around tree branches. These tails usually disappear before bones develop within them, so babies are born without them. But in a few, very rare cases, bones develop inside the tail, and a baby is born with a stubby tail that dangles from the tailbone (just above the bum).

People with tails? Really? That's so cool!
It's very rare (only twenty to thirty vestigial tails have been spotted in the last century), but it does happen.

Can I have one?
No.

Booo. Spoilsport.
Anyway, the point is – vestigial tails are the useless, shrivelled remains of an organ that once served a purpose, but is no longer of any use to the bearer.

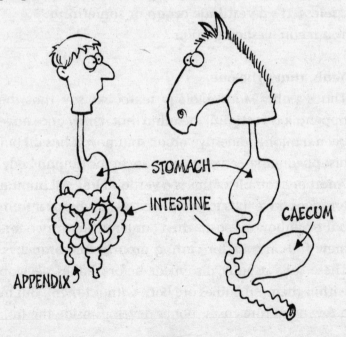

STOMACH

INTESTINE

CAECUM

APPENDIX

And for most of medical history the appendix has been thought of in the same way.

So what was it that the appendix used to do?

Most biologists believed that the appendix was once a kind of digestive organ called a **caecum**. In addition to stomachs, intestines and other digestive organs, birds, insects and other animals have these to store and digest tough leafy plant matter. This allows the animal to eat and store more food while on the move, so that they can continue hunting or grazing, and put off full digestion of the things they eat until later.

When anatomists and biologists first found the appendix, they failed to see what job it did in the digestive system. So they decided that it was probably *once* a bulging, bag-like crop, which helped our scavenging mammalian ancestors store tough, leafy plant matter for digestion. But as our diets changed from leafy plants to fruits, nuts, fish and meat, it was thought that the appendix was no longer needed, and it began to shrivel up and disappear. So much so, that by the time we evolved into modern humans, it looked more like a fat, stubby worm than a big, fleshy storage bag. It was considered a useless, 'extra' lump of flesh attached to the gut. (That's where it got its name – 'appendix' just means 'something attached' in Latin.)

The only thing the appendix *seemed* to do was make us ill when it got infected. An appendix infected with nasty bacteria causes **appendicitis**, in which the organ can swell up, burst and release the bacteria into the abdominal cavity. Left untreated, this can kill you. So at the first signs of appendicitis surgeons have tended to whip them out.* After all, if the appendix is useless anyway, why take the risk of leaving it in there?

But I'm guessing that's not the whole story, right?
Right. Biologists now believe that the appendix *does* have a purpose, so unless it's about to burst, we may be better off trying to treat the infection and leave the appendix in there.

Why do they think that?
Because if it were true that the appendix really had been shrivelling over millions of years, then you'd expect it to be bigger in the bodies of our animal ancestors than it is in the human body. But when – quite recently – a team of biologists looked at the appendixes of chimps, bonobos and gorillas (not our direct ancestors, but our closest living animal relatives), they found that it was even *smaller* and *more shrivelled* in those animals than it was in us! So, they figured, perhaps it's not useless after all. Perhaps it's now doing *something else* in the human body,

---

* This operation – called an **appendectomy** – is very common, so you probably have at least one person in your family who has had their appendix out. Just ask and see!

which would explain why it has stuck around.

So what does it do?
Whatever its original job was, it now looks as if the appendix is used to store bacteria, rather than food. You may remember from the last chapter that your intestines are home to billions of helpful bacteria, called gut flora. These are the famous 'good bacteria' you hear about in yoghurt adverts, which protect your gut lining from infection by 'bad' bacteria, and help you to digest your food by breaking down the tougher proteins, fats and starches within it. You inherit many of these helpful bugs from your mother, and they colonize your guts soon after you're born.

But if you're born with these good bugs, then why would you need to store more of them in your appendix?
Because certain illnesses – like stomach flu and food poisoning – can kill off your gut flora. If you suffer a nasty bout of diarrhoea (a symptom of these and other illnesses), you may lose most or all of them, and there's a danger of the 'bad' bugs moving in to take their place. But if you have an appendix, then you have a back-up store of 'good' bugs sealed off in a little pouch between your small and large intestines. From here, the 'good' bugs can migrate to the gut, and multiply to form new colonies throughout your intestines. And, while you can survive without an

appendix, you'll probably find it harder to recover from illnesses of the gut, and you'll be more vulnerable to getting infected all over again.

So it's not so much an 'extra thingy', as an 'extra handy thingy'.
Exactly.

Cool. Okay – one more thing . . .
What's that?

If I really *wanted* a tail, could they, like, stick one on me?
Good grief . . .

Do cats give you asthma?

No, they don't. If you already have asthma, cats can trigger asthma attacks. But they don't cause asthma in the first place. In fact, owning a cat can even prevent you from developing asthma. It all depends on your genes.

But my friend has asthma, and whenever she comes round to our house, our cats make her wheeze and she can't breathe properly.
Okay . . . and does she have cats at home?

Come to think of it, no.
There you go, then. While your cats may trigger your friend's asthma attacks, they didn't actually *give* her asthma in the first place, did they?

Asthma is a **chronic** (or long-term) **disease** of the airways (or **bronchial tubes**) which makes it difficult for sufferers to get air in and out of the lungs. Normally, air flows freely through these tubes from the nose and mouth, down through the trachea and into the bronchi and bronchioles of the lungs. But in an asthma sufferer (or **asthmatic**), the fleshy linings become swollen and produce a thick mucus which is difficult to shift. This partly closes the airways, making it harder to get air in and out.

In asthmatics, the airways also become very sensitive. When irritated, they may swell up further, blocking off the airways almost completely. This is

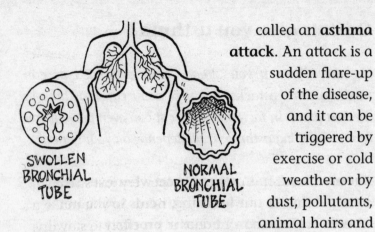

SWOLLEN
BRONCHIAL
TUBE

NORMAL
BRONCHIAL
TUBE

called an **asthma attack**. An attack is a sudden flare-up of the disease, and it can be triggered by exercise or cold weather or by dust, pollutants, animal hairs and other things found in the air we breathe.

Wait a minute – if animal hairs can give you an asthma attack, then doesn't that still mean cats can cause asthma?

Not quite, no. Because with asthma – and most other diseases – there's a big difference between the *cause* of a disease and the *triggers* of an attack.

I don't get it. Aren't they the same thing?

Look at it this way. Let's say you spend your whole life eating greasy bacon butties every morning, and twenty hamburgers for lunch and dinner. On top of all that, you smoke ten packets of cigarettes every day, and you refuse to do any kind of exercise. Live like this, and by the time you reach middle age (if you're lucky enough to survive that long), you shouldn't be surprised to find you've developed heart disease. The blood vessels leading to and from your heart will be clogged up with fatty goo, your blood pressure will be very high, and your heart will be under an enormous amount of strain, just trying to pump blood through your narrow arteries.

Okay. That figures. Now what?
Now let's say one day you decide to walk home from the fast-food shop in town. On the very last stretch of the trip home, it starts raining, hard. So you make a short dash for your front door in an effort to stay dry. In no time, your heartbeat gets faster and faster, and all of a sudden it stops altogether. You collapse, and a neighbour has to call an ambulance. If you're lucky, the ambulance arrives in time, and you're taken to the hospital to recover. So what just happened?

Errr . . . I had a heart attack.
Right. But what *caused* the heart attack? Was it the short jog? The rain?

Well . . . not really, no. It was all those years of smoking and slobbing.
Exactly. While the running may have *triggered* the heart *attack*, the *cause* of the heart *disease* was smoking, poor diet and a lack of exercise. The trigger and the cause are very different things.

So is that how it is with asthma too?
Sort of, yes. While exercise, cold weather and animal

hair can all trigger asthma attacks, none of these things actually cause asthma in the first place. Think about it – if they did, all Olympic athletes (along with cat owners, Swedes, Norwegians and Canadians) would be asthmatic.

So what *does* cause asthma?

To be honest, doctors and biologists don't yet know for sure. We know part of it is down to your genes – the DNA you inherit from your parents. Having certain faulty versions of genes leaves you with hypersensitive airways and thicker, stickier mucus in your lungs – which is the basis for developing asthma. But these faulty genes alone don't necessarily make you asthmatic. Often, certain things you're exposed to as a baby interact with the faulty genes to create full-blown asthma. These might include cigarette smoke (if your parents smoke), air pollution (if you live near a busy road, factory or power station), antibiotics, viruses and more.

Later, once your airways have become hypersensitive, you may become allergic to plant pollen, dust mites, cat hair or dog hair, and any one of these things might trigger an asthma attack. But again – like cold weather and exercise – these things may trigger flare-ups, but they're not actually causes of the disease. In fact, one study recently showed that having a cat in the house as a small child can cause your body to develop special antibodies that prevent allergic reactions to cats, and even prevent asthma attacks altogether.

So should I sniff my kitties as often as possible, to stop me from getting asthma?
Well, it doesn't quite work that way. Depending on your genes, exposure to cats (along with dogs, dust mites and pollen) may help develop immunity to them *or* make you allergic to them. And, without looking at your genes, you can't know for sure which way it'll go.

But look on the bright side – if you *do* end up having to give your cats away, it'd be the perfect excuse for buying a pet snake, lizard or tarantula. After all, no one's allergic to those.

Hmmm. Somehow I think my mum would be happier with the cats. One more thing, though . . .
What's that?

How do cats know when people are allergic to them?
Our cats don't like strangers, but they always jump right on to allergic people as soon as they sit down.

Ahh. Well, that could be because people who don't *want* cats sitting on them tend to avoid eye contact with cats. Eye contact makes some cats feel threatened, while avoiding eye contact is taken as a friendly signal.

Oh. Is that it, then?
Well, that and some cats are just *mean* . . .

What's more dangerous – bacteria or viruses?

That all depends on which species of virus or bacterium you're talking about. Most viruses and bacteria are actually harmless to humans. But some can be deadly, infecting and killing millions of people every year. And while bacterial diseases tend to be easier to treat, both types of microbe can be dangerous.

Hang on a minute – what's the difference between a bacterium and a bacteria?

'Bacterium' is the singular for 'bacteria'. So if you're talking about one, individual organism (or species), you call it a **bacterium**. If you're talking about lots of them, the plural word is **bacteria**. We use this, because the word 'bacterium' is Latin. And you can't say 'bacteriums' in Latin.

Okay, good. I'm glad we've got that sorted. Now what's the difference between a bacterium and a virus?

A bacterium is a single-celled, microscopic life-form (or **microbe**) that lives, feeds and reproduces all by itself. There are trillions upon trillions of bacteria on planet Earth. They are the most ancient and most numerous life forms on the planet. They've been around for at least 3.6 billion years – almost as long as the Earth itself. We've already discovered thousands of different species of bacteria, but the chances are there are hundreds of thousands of species – maybe even millions of species – still out there waiting to be found. A thousand different species live in your intestine alone!

So where do they live?

Pretty much everywhere. There are bacteria that live in the soil, in the air, in the ocean, in rivers and lakes. Bacteria have been found beneath the burning sands of the desert and within the ice sheets of the Arctic. And, of course, a good number of them live inside the bodies of animals, plants and other organisms.

The good news is that, of the many thousands of species of bacteria that surround us each day, less than one per cent seem to be harmful to us. Most – like the *staphylococci* bacteria that live on your skin, or the *lactobacillus* bacteria that live in your gut – just hang out there, eating spare skin cells and body wastes. Some even help you to survive by fighting off other, harmful bugs, and breaking down tough foods to release vitamins and minerals.

Unfortunately, that rare one per cent of harmful species includes some pretty nasty characters. Among them are the microbes that cause tetanus, typhoid, cholera, pneumonia, tuberculosis and bubonic plague.

Yikes! That's quite a line-up! Okay – so how are they different from viruses?

Viruses are microscopic parasites that are usually much smaller than bacteria – in fact, many of them live inside bacteria, in a similar way to how bacteria live inside us!

Well, I say, 'live', but in fact most biologists don't consider viruses to be alive. This is because a virus lacks the ability to reproduce all by itself. It has to hijack the microscopic copying machinery inside the cells of other (living) organisms in order to make copies of itself and spread itself around.

So why do these nasty bacteria and viruses make us sick?

The nasty microbes – of both types – are parasites. They invade our bodies and feed off the nutrients and energy our bodies provide. Harmful bacteria may multiply within a specific organ (like the heart or liver) or infect the entire bloodstream, drawing much-needed nutrients away from your body's own cells in the process. Some also release toxic chemicals, which destroy or paralyse nerves and muscles. If they aren't killed off by your immune system or medicines, they may destroy entire organs, prevent you from eating and moving, or cause so much water loss through vomiting and diarrhoea that your heart and brain stop functioning.

While the signs and symptoms can be just as nasty, the parasitic viruses that cause viral diseases work in slightly different ways. While plants and

VIRUS

CELL

VIRUS
INSIDE

VIRUS
MULTIPLYING

animals are **multi-celled** and bacteria are **single-celled**, viruses are 'no-celled'. They're basically just bits of information (coded in strings of DNA, or sometimes in a related type of chemical called RNA) surrounded by a protein coat. When a virus encounters a cell, the coat proteins stick to the outside of the cell, and the cell envelops it, drawing the virus inside.

Once there, the virus inserts itself into the cell's **nucleus** (where the cell's own DNA is copied), and the cell unwittingly makes thousands of copies of the virus, using its own nutrients and energy to do so. Once built, the army of new viral particles bursts out of the cell and infects the cells around it. When this happens to lots of cells in the same tissue or organ, the whole thing starts to shut down. If your body fails to fight the virus off, the tissues, organs and systems may shut down altogether. So although viruses are smaller and simpler than bacteria, the dangerous ones are every bit as nasty.

So which one is easier to get rid of?
Again, that depends on which species of bacterium or virus you're dealing with. In general, bacteria tend to

be easier to treat. We can use **antiseptics** (like bleach and antiseptic soap) to stop bacteria growing on skin and wounds in the first place. And, once they're inside the body, we can treat most of them with **antibiotics** – chemicals (often from plants and fungi) that stop bacteria from reproducing. Viruses, on the other hand, don't respond to antibiotics. So they tend to be a bit trickier to deal with.

But why don't antibiotics work on viruses?
Because antibiotics target the bits of living machinery inside bacterial cells that the bacterium uses to copy itself and reproduce. But, if you remember, viruses aren't alive, so they don't use their own copying machinery – they use *ours*. And since we can't shut down our *own* copying machinery without killing our *own cells* too, we generally have to wait it out and hope for the best. There are a few types of drug (called **antivirals**), which target other bits of the virus, and stop its reproduction in other ways. And of course there are vaccines,* which help your body to recognize and fight off certain types of virus. But, for the most part, you just have to wait, rest and hope your immune system eventually takes care of it.

For the most part, your body does this job very well. When you're infected with a virus, your immune

---

* For more about these, see 'Can injections give you diseases?' on page 123.

system will usually destroy it within twenty-four to forty-eight hours. You might feel rough while it does the job, but once it's done, you're back to full health. Elderly people and young babies, however, have weaker or less developed immune systems, making them more vulnerable to viruses. That's why we give vaccines to babies and older folks, to protect them against common viral diseases like measles and the flu.

But what happens if you get infected by a *really nasty* one, and you can't get rid of it?
Well, then you're in for a lot more trouble. For a short list of nasty bugs you really want to avoid, check out the Top 10 Microscopic Nasties opposite.

In no particular order, here are the ten nastiest bacterial and viral diseases in the world today. Read 'em and weep.

1) **Bubonic plague**. Known in medieval times as the Black Death, this famous plague is caused by the bacterium *Yersina pestis*, which hangs out in the bloodstream of the fleas found on rats. When the plague first hit Europe in 1340, it killed over 25 million people. When it returned in 1665, it killed a fifth of the population of London. The last known outbreak was in 2006, when fifty people died in the Democratic Republic of the Congo, Africa.

2) **Flu**. Caused by the shape-shifting **influenza virus**, flu kills tens of thousands of elderly people each year. In the last great influenza outbreak of 1918, between 50 and 100 million people were killed worldwide in a little over twelve months. For this reason, scientists are always keeping an eye out for nasty new strains.

3) **Tuberculosis**. TB is caused by a bacterium called *Mycobacterium tuberculosis* which infects and destroys the lungs, but can also settle in – and severely damage – bones, brains and other parts of the body. The bacterium spreads through droplets that are coughed, sneezed or spat into the air and inhaled by the unlucky sufferer. It is estimated that a third of the world's population (over 2 billion people) are infected with TB, and the disease kills millions every year.

4) Measles. Measles is a highly contagious disease caused by the **rubeola virus**, which infects the lungs and results in fevers, rashes, coughing and sneezing. It usually clears up by itself within a week or so, but in some (rare) cases, it can cause blindness, brain damage and even death. Measles still kills over 160,000 children a year worldwide, most of them in developing countries, which is one reason why the vaccine (part of the MMR vaccine given to children in the UK and other countries) is so important.

5) Smallpox. The **variola virus** causes smallpox, a very nasty infectious disease that kills around a third of its victims. In the eighteenth century alone, smallpox killed over 60 million Europeans, including several kings and queens. Thankfully, though, thanks to a global vaccination programme, smallpox seem to have been eradicated from the planet altogether, and only survives in a few research labs worldwide.

6) Cholera. Caused by the bacterium *Vibrio cholerae*, cholera is transmitted through infected water, and causes extreme diarrhoea that, without treatment, can kill you in as little as four hours. Although it's rare in the developed world, it still kills hundreds of people every year and an epidemic can kill thousands.

7) Ebola. The terrifying **Ebola virus** causes death to 80–90 per cent of everyone it infects. Worse yet, it does it by liquefying your organs and causing bleeding from your eyes, ears and skin sores. Thankfully, it's not actually that infectious and is very rare outside of select regions of Africa.

8) **HIV/AIDS**. AIDS, or Acquired Immunodeficiency Syndrome, is caused by the **human immunodeficiency virus**, or **HIV**. Around 40 million people are infected with HIV worldwide, and the virus causes 1–5 million deaths every year. AIDS can be treated but at present there is no cure.

9) **Pneumonia**. Caused by a variety of bacteria AND viruses, pneumonia is a disease of the lungs and respiratory tract that is responsible for millions of deaths every year, including half of all fatalities among elderly people. Among younger people, only those with HIV/AIDS or another immune disease are usually at risk.

10) **Whooping cough**. Infection with the bacterium *Bordetella pertussis* leads to whooping cough, a disease of the lungs that gets its name from the uncontrollable coughing it causes. Although it can be treated with antibiotics, it still causes over 300,000 childhood deaths each year. (I nearly died of this myself when I was two years old.)

Could you make candles out of earwax?

It's possible, yes. But it would take you a very long time, and they would smell so bad you would most likely wish you hadn't bothered. Earwax is actually a kind of modified sweat, which forms a sticky protective layer inside your ear canal. And if you ask me it's best left where it is.

Earwax is solid, sticky sweat? Urrrghhh!

Kind of, yes. Like sweat, earwax (or **cerumen**) is made of fatty acids and oils mixed together with dead skin cells, hair and more than a few dead bacteria. As such, it's perhaps not the loveliest material to make candles out of. Unless, of course, you're making a present for someone you really don't like.

Where does it come from?

Cerumen is made in **sebaceous** and **cerumenous glands** that line the outer **ear canal** (the bit between your actual lughole and the eardrum, which marks the boundary with the middle and inner ear). Once it has oozed out of the glands, fresh earwax forms a soft, yellow layer that covers most of the ear canal. But as it ages and decays it dries out and turns brown, black or white.[*]

---

[*] The colour (and softness) depend on your genes. For more about how this works, see the 'Ears Around the World' box at the end of this section.

Gross! So what's it *doing* in there?

Earwax forms a protective layer atop the soft, delicate skin of your ear canal. Your eardrums sense sound waves as waves of changing air pressure. But to do this the ear canals leading to them have to remain open to the wind, air and world outside. This soon leaves them coated with dust and dirt, and makes them vulnerable to infection by nasty bacteria just waiting for a chance to get in there.

A healthy layer of sticky earwax traps dust and dirt, and helps to shield the ear lining and eardrum from infection. Bugs and grime become trapped in the sticky wax, which then dries out and tumbles out of your ears in dry, crusty flakes. (Don't worry – they're usually so small that no one will notice this cascading ear poo.) Some people produce more earwax than others, and may have to wipe the outer parts of their ears once every few days to clear them of wax flakes. But, for most of us, the ears are handy, self-cleaning organs, and we can leave them to take care of themselves.

Still sounds pretty gross to me. Couldn't I just scrape all my earwax out for a proper cleaning?

That's not the best idea, as it could actually be very bad for your ears. If you scrape out your earwax, it can no longer do its job of protecting your ears from infection. Worse yet, scraping and prodding around inside your ears with cotton buds and such can crush and compact your earwax. When this happens, fresh oils from the glands below can no longer get into the wax, and it hardens into a crust. These slabs of compacted wax can cause a lot of pain, and if they form on your eardrum they can even lead to hearing loss. So, like I said, you're better off just keeping the outsides of your ears clean, and leaving the insides well alone.

But if you *could* scoop out all your earwax without hurting yourself . . . could you make it into a candle?

Well, you *could*, I suppose. But since most ears produce little more than a teaspoonful of wax each week it would take up to a year to collect enough to make a 15 cm candle. And after all that effort you might wish you'd never bothered. With so many impurities (like ear hairs and dead skin cells) inside, the candle wouldn't burn very evenly. It would pop, crackle and spit all over the place. And since earwax is essentially oozed from lughole sweat glands, frankly, the smell would be pretty terrible. You know those aromatherapy candles that fill the house with the smell of vanilla, lavender or orange blossom? Well, imagine that – only these ones smell like sweaty armpits, old socks and cheesy belly buttons.

Ewwwww! Yuck! But that can't be right. I mean, I've seen 'ear wax candles' on sale in the

shops, and on the Internet. If they smell that bad, why would anyone buy one? Ahh, but those 'earwax candles' aren't actually 'candles made of earwax'. They're 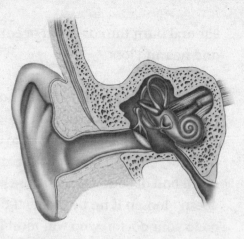 candles made for *removing* earwax. Or at least that's what they are *supposed* to do.

'Earwax candles' are used in **ear-candling**, which is an alternative medicine treatment for extra, built-up earwax. The idea is that you lie on your side, stick a long, hollow 'earwax candle' in your ear, and burn it until it's about two to five centimetres from your lughole. This is supposed to create a vacuum that magically sucks excess earwax and 'toxins' out of your ear and up into the hollow candle.

Does that work?

No. According to most doctors, ear-candling is a useless treatment, and can also be dangerous and harmful to your ears. Nothing actually comes out of your ear during candling – the black stuff left inside the candle afterwards is just soot from the burning candle itself. But, unfortunately, stuff may get in. If you're not careful, hot wax may drip down into the ear and burn the ear canal or eardrum, causing pain and hearing loss.

That's crazy! So what *should* I do if my ears get really bunged up with wax?

Your best bet is to get someone to dribble a little warm (not hot) olive oil into your ear, and plug it up with a small ball of cotton wool before you go to bed. If that doesn't loosen it up by the next day, then you should go to your doctor, who will most likely break the wax up by blasting it out with a water-filled syringe. This doesn't hurt, but it does sound a bit like someone just unleashed a waterfall inside your head!

Does the doctor let you keep your earwax afterwards?

Errr . . . not usually, no. Why do you ask?

Well, I have this horrible auntie, and I'd really like to make her a Christmas present this year . . .

Can injections give you diseases?

If by 'injections' you mean 'vaccines', then not really, no. Vaccines are designed to protect you from disease, and although some do involve injecting you with viruses or bacteria, they're strictly tested for safety for many years before they're given to everyday people.

What? **Some injections actually have viruses in them? That's crazy! What are they trying to do to us?**

Whoa, whoa, whoa! Slow down there. Yes, some types of vaccine do feature real bacteria and viruses. Sometimes, they're even versions of the things you're trying to protect yourself against. But they don't do you any harm, as they're deactivated before they're used. So it's all good.

All good, my foot! I'm not having some nurse inject a virus into me! No way!

Okay – let's start this from the beginning. Do you even know what a vaccine is?

Yes. Of course I do. It's an injection they give you to stop you getting a disease. Like measles, or flu, or TB . . .

That's correct. Some vaccines – like the measles, mumps and rubella (MMR) vaccine, you get when you're a baby. Others, like the BCG jab that combats tuberculosis (or TB), you get later on. But do you know what's actually *in* these injections?

Errr . . . I dunno. Medicine? Antibiotics?
Not quite. A medicine is any chemical that has a useful effect on the body – they're used to prevent inflammation, kill pain, lower fevers and so on. An antibiotic is a specific type of medicine that stops bacteria from growing. (So antibiotics can be used to fight bacterial infections, but are useless against viruses and viral diseases like flu.)

But vaccines are a bit different. Vaccines are actually preparations of living or dead micro-organisms (bacteria or viruses), which are given to a patient in order to trigger an immune response. So, in a way, vaccines encourage the body to create its *own* medicines – in the form of immune cells and antibodies – so that it can better fight infections and diseases by itself.

But doesn't that make you ill? I mean, I get the idea, but isn't giving someone bacteria and viruses a bit on the risky side?
No, it isn't, because to remove the risk of real infection and illness, the bacteria and viruses are made harmless in the process of creating the vaccine. Some vaccine bugs are treated with certain chemicals which make them unable to reproduce or invade cells. Others are cut into pieces, and only their outer

coat proteins (the bits the immune system recognizes) are injected as a vaccine.

Whenever you're infected with a harmful microbe (a bacterium or virus), white blood cells and antibodies recognize the outer coat of the bug, latch on to it and signal other immune cells to come as reinforcements. In most cases, these back-up cells then kill off the invading bugs, and you recover from the disease. How long it takes to recover (or whether you recover at all) depends on how easily and quickly your immune cells recognize the bug as an enemy.

If you've been infected by the same microbe before (let's say you've already had chickenpox, which is caused by the varicella zoster virus), then special memory cells remain in your blood and tissues after the infection. So if you're infected again these cells quickly spot the varicella zoster virus and signal other cells to kill it almost immediately. As a result, you do not develop chickenpox again. You are now **immune** to chickenpox.

Vaccines take advantage of this clever memory system by infecting you with safe, harmless versions of nasty microbes which *look* like the real thing, but don't actually invade your cells or cause damage to your body. Real or not, your immune cells spot the vaccine bug, destroy it and leave memory cells on guard for a future infection. So even if you've never been infected by that bug before, you'll now be *immune* to it, ahead of time. Genius.

But don't some people feel ill after getting injections? And I heard that some of those baby injections can give them brain diseases later on.
It's true that some people feel queasy after vaccines. But this is usually just a side effect that happens as their bodies start to react to the vaccine and make protective immune cells and antibodies. They're not actually coming down with flu or measles, or whatever. A few people are also allergic to certain chemicals or vaccines, so they may get ill after receiving them. For this reason, you're usually tested before getting 'big' vaccines like TB, to make sure your body can handle it first.

As for baby vaccines and brain diseases, that story has been going around since the early 1990s, after one doctor claimed that the MMR jab was causing autism (a brain condition that a small number of children are born with each year). But he had no real proof that it was happening, and no one has found any solid evidence of it since. All that's happened since then is that lots of frightened parents have refused to give their babies MMR vaccines, and – sadly – thousands of children have suffered with measles, mumps and rubella because they weren't protected.

That's really sad.
Yes, it is. And the truly sad thing is that there's no reason for this. We *know* the vaccines we use are safe, because they're tested in laboratories for years – decades, even – before doctors are allowed to give them to ordinary people in surgeries and hospitals. Thanks to vaccines, we've wiped out the disease smallpox worldwide, and there are far fewer cases of polio, rubella and other diseases in the countries that vaccinate against them. Vaccines are a massive success story in the history of medicine. And yet many people still avoid them, because of scary stories in newspapers and Internet articles.

Well, because of that and also because vaccinations involve big pointy needles jabbing into you.
Hmmmm. Good point. But look at it this way: which would you rather have – one brief second of pain and a 'dead arm' . . . or several months of pain and a dead everything when you develop a disease like TB?

Ah. Gotcha. Okay, gimme the jab.
A fine choice, sir. And I may I recommend the large needle with the scary-looking end?

Erk.

Crossword puzzle: microbes and immunity

Solve the clues in this tricky crossword puzzle and test your knowledge of bugs, diseases and the immune system. Answers on page 235.

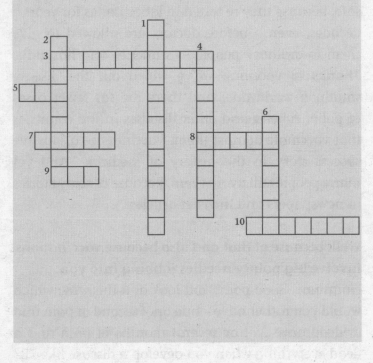

Across

3 A type of medicine or drug which stops bacteria from reproducing

5 A place inside your body where lactobacillus bacteria live

7 Antibiotics don't work on this type of microbe

8 A rare but deadly virus, found in parts of Africa, which liquefies in your organs!

9 A shorter way of referring to the measles, mumps and rubella vaccine

10 A disease caused by the rubeola virus, which gives you the fevers, spots and rashes

Down

1 A disease of the lungs caused by the bacterium *Bordetella pertussis*, which Glenn nearly died of as a baby

2 A single-celled, living organism, which may or may not cause disease

4 A disease caused by the varicella zoster virus

6 A medicine created from deactivated microbes, which makes you immune to a specific disease

THE JAB DODGER

Why do bug bites itch?

Because they trigger the release of chemicals beneath the skin that cause swelling, itching and allergic reactions. The itchy feeling itself travels through special nerves (or 'itch fibres') to the spine and brain. It's these 'itchy signals' that make you want to scratch so badly!

So bugs inject you with itchy chemicals to make you scratch?

Not exactly, no. The 'itchy chemicals' are actually made inside your body. When a bug bite pierces the skin, it triggers the release of a chemical called **histamine** within your skin tissues. Histamine causes **inflammation** of the skin and other tissues, which usually helps with healing and repair. When histamine is release in a damaged tissue, it causes blood vessels to widen and become leaky, bringing nutrients, red blood cells and white blood cells to the area to help fight infection and rebuild the tissue.

It also triggers pain signals in nearby nerve endings, which tell your brain (to tell you) that you've been cut, bitten or damaged in some way, and to be careful with that bit of your body while it heals up. As the wound heals, the pain signals fade to a dull itch – annoying enough to tell you the wound is still there, but not painful enough to stop you from getting on with things.

So an itch is really just a tiny stab of pain? A reminder of an injury that hasn't quite healed up?

In some cases, yes. But in others – such as bug bites – the system goes a bit crazy. If the cells that release histamine become too sensitive, then histamine can be released too easily (or too much of it released for too long). When that happens, even a tiny bug bite, or a scratch from a woolly jumper fibre – can trigger redness, swelling and the kind of crazy itching that makes you want to chop your own leg off.

But why do we even itch at all? I mean, what's the point of it?

Biologists don't know for sure, but there are few ideas as to why itching and scratching may sometimes come in handy.

Sometimes – as with bug bites – an itch is a warning that your skin has been pierced or damaged. In the first instance, this tells you to remove (i.e. squish or pick out) the mosquito or tick before it does much more damage. Later, the itch may serve as a reminder to be careful with that area – to keep it clean, avoid touching it and so on – until it has fully healed. An itch may also be a warning against touching or eating certain toxic plants, like stinging nettles and poison ivy. In this case, the plant has evolved chemicals in its leaves that trigger a massive release of histamine when the leaves graze your skin. It's a sneaky self-defence mechanism evolved by the plant, which says, 'Warning: do not touch (or else).'

On the other hand, an itch may also *encourage* you to touch and scratch your skin. Itching after sunburn, for example, stimulates a scratch that helps to remove old dead, flaky skin, revealing the fresh, healthy skin underneath. And it's possible that some insects and bacteria trigger itching and scratching in an effort to make you rub your skin raw. This brings more blood to the area (on which a sneaky flea or tick may feed), and creates larger patches of soft, bloody sores for bacteria to invade and breed upon.

Yuck! So my mum's right, then – if I scratch an itch, I'm probably only making it worse?
In many cases, yes. It's usually best just to ignore an itch. If you can stop scratching it for more than six to eight minutes, it'll often stop itching all by itself. Scratching just brings more blood (and histamine) to the area, and prolongs the agony.

So why does scratching an itch feel so good, then? Sometimes, that makes an itch go away. At least for a while.
Right. That's because the itch signal travels to your brain via sensory nerves in your skin. Bug bites and woolly jumpers trigger nerves that carry both 'itch' and 'pain' signals. So if you scratch, pinch, rub or heat up the itchy region, the pain signal can temporarily

override the itch signal, and the itch goes away (at least for a minute or so).

But sometimes this works, and sometimes it doesn't. That's because there's a second type of sensory nerve – one just discovered by scientists – that carries only 'itch' signals. Since these nerves aren't affected by pain, they just keep on itching. It's these nerves that cause the itching you get with eczema, and many diseases of the skin, liver and immune system. This type of itching can go on for months or years and can only be treated with special medicines. Some plants can create itches like this too, so be careful what you brush against when you're walking through woods or forests!

Ichkkkk! This is making me itchy just thinking about it.
It's funny you should say that, as part of itching (and the relief we get from scratching an itch) is also in your head. If you think about an itch, it becomes much worse. In fact, you can even generate an itch with thoughts alone.

What? You're having me on.
No, really – it's true. Try this on for size:

Imagine that while you're reading this book, a scuttling swarm of ticks, ants and beetles crawl out from under the floor, up the side of the chair you're sitting on and into your underwear. And there

they are, right now
– crunching and
scuttling around
in your undies,
crawling up
your bottom . . .

. . . and now a pair of centipedes
is making its way up your belly, scuttling into your
armpits, up your back, around your neck, into your
ears . . .

Arggghhhhh! Enough! Stop it! I'm itchy all over!
Heheheheh! Told ya.

Why do sweaty feet stink?

Actually, sweaty feet don't stink at all. It's the sweat-eating bacteria that live on them that smell so bad. That delightful, distinctive odour of cheesy feet is released from bugs left to grow inside your stinky socks and shoes.

Sweat-eating bacteria that live on your feet? *Gross!*
Believe me, it gets worse. These sweat-eating bugs aren't just confined to your feet. They're all over your body. The average adult has a total skin area of around two square metres. And on that skin live over 1,000 species of bacteria, from up to twenty different biological families (or, rather, **phyla**).

That's the most disgusting thing I've ever heard. Tell me more. What are they *doing* there?
For the most part, they're just hanging out – eating and drinking the sweat, skin oil, dead skin cells and other wastes that build up on the surface of your body. It's like one big bacterial party.

Isn't that dangerous? I mean, don't bacteria give you diseases?
Some of them do, yes. But most of the 'bug' species that commonly live on human skin – such as corynebacteria, micrococci, and staphylococci – are pretty harmless. And even the ones that can do

us harm are kept safely at bay by the solid, fleshy barrier of the skin itself. Once in a while, though, they can (quite literally) get under your skin and cause problems. If you suffer a nasty cut, graze or burn, bacteria can slip in through the break in your skin's defences and form a bacterial invasion (or **infection**).

. . . and then you have to take antibiotics, right?

Well, even when this invasion does happen, your immune cells usually fight the bugs off by themselves. It's only when these immune cells fail, and the infection threatens to hang around, or spread to your bloodstream, that doctors have to attack them with antibiotic drugs. And, in fact, antibiotics don't typically kill the bacteria either. They just stop them growing or feeding for a while, which gives the body's own immune cells a chance to call for reinforcements and mount a counter-attack.

So if all these bugs are feeding on our sweat, why do we sweat at all?

Well, sweat is a major part of your body's temperature control system. One function of your skin is to insulate your body, and stop it from getting too hot or cold. But it also uses

HAIR → SKIN SURFACE SWEAT PORE SWEAT GLAND

special structures – like hairs and sweat glands – to control your inner body temperature when things get a little extreme.

When your body temperature drops – such as when you're caught outside in cold weather without a jacket – hairs embedded in the skin stand up to trap a layer of warm air near the skin. This prevents heat loss from the body, keeping you warm and toasty inside. But when your body temperature rises – for example when you're exercising or lounging on the beach under a blazing sun – you need to lose heat, not retain it. So sweat glands deep beneath the skin release droplets of water on to the surface through tiny tubes or **sweat ducts**. Once there, these wet droplets evaporate, taking some extra heat with them.

So sweaty skin *does* have a purpose. It helps cool your body down.

So why is it just sweaty *feet* that stink?
Well, there are a few other stinky areas I can think of . . .

Okay – sweaty feet and armpits, then. You know what I mean. People don't usually have stinky knees or foreheads, do they?
Good point. Well, there are a couple of reasons for that. The first is that there are two different types of sweat gland in the body – called **eccrine** and **apocrine** glands. Eccrine sweat glands are found all over the

138

body, from the scalp to the soles of the feet. They release a clear, watery kind of sweat to help regulate body temperature. Apocrine glands are found only in your armpits and – ahem – nether regions. They produce a thick, milky, yellowish sweat rich in proteins and fats, partly to expel waste chemicals from the body and partly to communicate your own particular odour to other people. (Other animals use these smells to attract partners, but biologists are still arguing about whether this works the same way in humans!)

Unfortunately, the rich, milky apocrine-gland sweat in your armpits is also particularly tasty to bacteria, which helpfully munch on your proteins and release stinky chemicals as waste (i.e. stinky sweat = bug farts). *This* explains why armpit sweat smells different from, say, forehead sweat. And it also explains why we tend to apply deodorants (chemicals that mask or absorb stinky sweat smells) to our armpits but not our foreheads.

Hang on – that still doesn't explain why feet stink.
You're right, it doesn't. Or why some people's feet are stinkier than others. The simple answer to that one is

this: some people sweat more than others, and some people wash their socks more often than others.

While the eccrine-gland sweat released from your feet isn't particularly tasty to bacteria, if there's enough of it, the bugs will still bring the party to your trainers. If several days' worth of foot-sweat is trapped in the warm, cosy confines of an unwashed pair of socks or trainers, then the bacteria build up, and their stinky, cheese-smelling waste products build up along with them. And since some people sweat more than others, some people – and I'm not saying it's you, necessarily – should change their socks more often. At least, if they want to avoid being called Captain Reekyfeet . . .

GET IT SORTED: SWEATY STUFF

- The average adult has almost 3 million sweat glands, which are found more or less everywhere on the body except for the lips and nipples.

- In a warm climate, you can sweat 2–3 litres of water every hour!

- Sufferers of the disease **chromhidrosis** have malfunctioning sweat glands which produce multi-coloured sweat, in shades including red, blue, green, yellow and black.

Where do zits come from?

They start beneath your skin, when oil glands get clogged up and infected with bacteria. Then, as the bacteria grow and your body tries to fight them off, the zit swells, bulges and bursts through the surface of your skin. Zits are a real pain but most people get them and they usually don't last for long.

Ewww! Gross. Zits are oily bugs growing beneath your skin? So how do they get under there?

Well, the surface of your skin is home to millions of bacteria,* which feed on your dead skin cells and an oily goo called **sebum**, which squeezes out from special glands beneath the skin, called **sebaceous glands**. Usually, these skin bugs do you no harm. They just hang out – eating and multiplying – and their numbers are kept down by changing temperatures, radiation from the sun and regular rinsing with soap and water. But if the channels (or **pores**) that lead from the glands to the surface of your skin get clogged up with dead skin cells, then the oil can't get out. The oily skin cells begin to rot beneath the surface, making a lovely, warm, tasty environment for the skin bugs to invade and breed in. So, they do.

---

* See 'Why do sweaty feet stink?' on page 136, for more about skin flora.

But they don't just stay beneath the skin, do they? If that was it, you wouldn't have to worry, cos your zits would be invisible.

That's right, they don't. As the bugs multiply and feed inside the clogged pore, they swell up into a ball-shaped colony, and the skin above turns red as the surrounding skin tissue reacts to the invasion with **inflammation**. Blood vessels around the growing zit open up, bringing white blood cells to the area to help fight the infection. As this happens, the growing ball of bacteria, white blood cells and oily sebum nudges its way through the surface of the skin, with oh-so-appealing results . . .

If the infection is small, a **pimple** forms – just a small red lump at the surface, which usually disappears within a day or so as the infection is fought off. If the growing pus-ball gets a bit bigger, it forms a dome-shaped **whitehead** at the surface – the white colour coming from the white blood cells and bacteria densely packed inside.*

What about blackheads? Are they just dirty whiteheads?

Not quite. Dirt on the skin has little effect on zits, one way or the other. Blackheads are formed when pores are only partly clogged, and some sebum oil still oozes

---

* If you want to see this for yourself, pop an oily whitehead on to a glass slide and put it under a microscope to take a peek. Just make sure no one sees you doing it. It may be science, but it's still gross.

past the swollen bacterial pus-ball to reach the surface. When the sebum reacts with oxygen it turns black, adding an icky, inky cap to your prize zit.

WHITEHEAD

PIMPLE

BLACKHEAD

So if dirt doesn't cause zits, then what does?

A combination of things. Your genes (the DNA you inherit from each of your parents) have a bit to do with it, as they control the thickness and make-up of your skin oils. Diet and climate can affect zit formation too. If you don't get the right nutrients (especially vitamin A and essential fatty acids), then your skin cells can get too sticky. And if old skin cells aren't exposed to sunlight and removed by wind, rain and washing, they may clog pores more easily. And, perhaps most importantly, hormones – special proteins that rise and fall as you go through puberty and other growth periods – may also affect the oiliness of your skin in a big way.

This is why around 80 per cent of people aged ten to thirty have zits at one time or another. Almost everybody gets them when they go through puberty. (Boys often get worse zit outbreaks than girls, as their hormone levels swing up and down more wildly).

So how do you get rid of them?

Well, if you're prone to zits – or going through the age when you get them fairly often – you can help prevent zit outbreaks by eating a healthy diet, getting outside for sunshine, fresh air and exercise, and washing with a medicated, anti-bacterial lotion. Once you've got them, just keep doing the same and wait it out. If they get really bad, your doctor may prescribe antibiotics to help stop the bacteria growing. But this is usually only for really bad, constant outbreaks. And for most people the zit lotions and washes will do the job just as well.

What about popping and squeezing them? Will that help?

For the most part, no. Although it may feel good (and temporarily get rid of the white stuff on a whitehead), squeezing often just irritates the sensitive nerves around them (making them sore and itchy) and adds more grimy bacteria from your fingertips, so that it takes longer for the infection to clear up. So, if you can, leave 'em alone.

Okay – one last thing . . .
What's that?

How do zits know to explode all over your face right before a crucial party or a school photo?
Ahh – now that's a mystery. It could be because you

get stressed at the thought of it, and that affects your hormones. Or maybe the zits just have a mind of their own . . .

5. All Skin and Bones

If you can break a bone, could you snap a muscle?

Yes, you can. But this rarely happens as it's very difficult to do, because special sensors inside stop you from snapping, ripping or tearing your muscles on purpose. In any case, if you do break a bone or tear a muscle, the injury will usually heal up all by itself.

Don't be silly. Bones don't repair themselves.

Yes, they do.

They don't.

All right, then – how do *you* think broken bones get repaired?

Well, *doctors* do it, don't they. With X-rays and plaster casts and stuff.

Ah, but it's not the doctors, X-rays or plaster casts that *do* the healing. X-rays allow doctors to look inside the body and see which bones (if any) are broken. If there *is* a break, then the doctor simply nudges* the bone back into place, and the bone begins to repair itself.

---

* If it's a *really* bad break, doctors or surgeons sometimes have to insert metal pins or screws into the bones to hold them in place while they heal. But most of the time this isn't necessary, and all they have to do is push the bone back into place and hold it there while the nurse wraps the area in bandages and plaster.

New bone tissue grows to seal the split (or **fracture**) within weeks, without any help from doctors, nurses or anyone else.

So what's the plaster cast for, then?

The plaster cast simply holds the bones still so that they can carry out their amazing self-repair job undisturbed. In fact, in some parts of Asia, doctors don't even apply plaster casts to broken bones. They just align the bones, tell the patient not to use the broken limb, and send 'em home. After that, they simply check in every week or so to make sure the bones are healing straight.

Seriously? That actually works?

As long as the break isn't too serious (like a completely shattered bone, or a **compound fracture** that pushes a snapped bit of bone through the skin), then yes – absolutely. Left alone to do its job, a broken bone will happily heal itself. Your bones, you see, are constantly regrowing and reshaping themselves throughout your lifetime. Special bone-building cells called **osteoblasts** are creating new bone tissue all the time, regrowing the bone from the inside out. Meanwhile, special bone-eating cells called **osteoclasts** are constantly munching away at your bone tissue – removing old, dead bone cells and maintaining the shape of the bone by chiselling away at the edges like tiny microscopic sculptors.

These bone-builders and bone-eaters remodel your bones throughout your entire lifetime. In fact, within seven years, every bone cell in your body has been regrown and replaced. So if you're over seven years old, you have a completely different skeleton from the one you were born with. And if you're over fourteen, you've regrown your entire skeleton twice!

No way!

Yes, way. So, you see, your bones are repairing themselves all the time. Breaking a bone simply kicks this process into emergency overdrive. Here's how it works:

Let's say you forget to wear your shin pads to football practice, and a nasty tackle breaks your **fibula** – the smaller of the two bones in your lower leg. The bone has snapped in the middle, but the two halves are still held more or less in place by the muscles and fibrous tissues all around them. The bone itself is a hollow tube, with hard bone tissue on the outside and fleshier **bone marrow** on the inside. Right away – before you've even been stretchered off the pitch – severed blood vessels within the marrow start to form a fleshy clot.

Provided that the split ends of your bones aren't too widely separated, this sticky blob will hold them in place all the way to the hospital. When you get there, the doctor orders an X-ray to check the damage. If the ends or edges of the bone are still out of place, the doctor pushes them together again (ouch), and a new clot forms as they meet. Otherwise, the doctor or nurse will simply hold the bones in place (by pressing on the sides of your leg) while they wrap the leg in bandages soaked in gooey liquid plaster.* When the plaster hardens into a cast, it will hold the bones in place for several weeks or months while the healing continues.

So then what happens?

After a week or so, special bone-marrow cells called **chondroblasts** replace the gooey clot holding the bone ends together with tough **collagen** fibres. This forms a knobbly, **fibrous callus**. This is tougher than the sticky clot, but still not strong enough to bear weight. Over the following weeks and months, osteoblasts (bone-builders) move into the callus and start to replace the collagen fibres with new bone tissue. On an X-ray, the break now looks like one

---

* Many hospitals now create casts using fibreglass bandages or special, heat-sensitive plastics instead. Depends where you go.

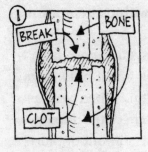

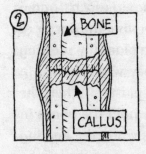

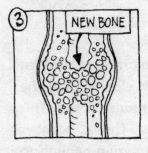

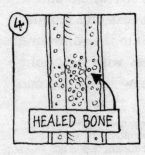

bone with a big ball or bulge in the middle. Finally, osteoclasts (bone-eaters) chew away at the edges of the bulge until the bone looks like one thin, straight shin bone again. Within two to three months the bone will be fully healed, and you can start walking on it once more (although it might be a while longer before you can run and play football, since the muscles waste away inside the casts and need strengthening before you're back to your full abilities).

That's cool. It's like superhero super-healing or something. So do ripped muscles heal the same way?

Torn muscles are a little simpler, although they can take just as long to heal as broken bones and may need extra help to get back into shape. It's rare that a whole muscle will be torn, as there are little sensory organs within each one – called Golgi organs – that prevent you from stretching them to breaking point. It's usually the thinner tendons* at the ends that tear first. But if the muscle is pulled very powerfully and suddenly while tense (this sometimes happens as a defender's boot clashes with the swinging thigh of a striker in football), the belly of the muscle can rip, causing a very painful injury.

Right away, the muscle forms a clot at the torn edges, and within a week collagen fibres grow to knit the ends together with tough scar tissue – in a similar way that the fibrous callus forms in bone. This 'heals' the muscle, but leaves it tight, inflexible and likely to rip again in other places. After that, it takes many months of exercise and physiotherapy for the scar tissue to be replaced with new, flexible muscle fibres. Eventually, though, this will happen, and you can jog back on to the pitch once more.

So, if I hurt my leg or ankle playing football, how do I know if it's a broken bone or a ripped muscle?

Like I said, ripped and torn muscles are rare. If you do twist your ankle or leg on the pitch, the chances are you've just strained or sprained a muscle or tendon. (This is when the muscle or tendon gets overstretched, but doesn't actually tear or snap). A good quick

---

* See 'What do double-jointed people look like on X-rays?' on page 154 for more about tendons.

check is to push *gently* on the end of an injured limb – whether it's a toe, ankle, leg, finger, wrist or arm – just hold it straight and press very gently in towards your body. If it's just strained, it'll be sore but not unbearable. If it's broken, it'll feel like someone just set fire to it, and it's off to the hospital for you.

Yeah, but then I'd get a cool plaster cast, and all my mates could sign it.
That's true. But, believe me, it's not worth it. Just wear your shin pads.

Top 10 commonly broken bones*

1) Wrist
2) Clavicle (or collarbone)
3) Hip
4) Finger
5) Toe
6) Foot
7) Ankle
8) Arm
9) Nose
10) Jaw

---

* Not in perfect order, since not all broken fingers and toes are reported or treated in hospital, and different age groups tend to break different bones. In people over seventy-five, the hip in the most common break. In young children it's the collarbone, and so on.

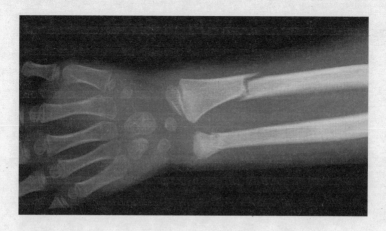

Top 10 bone-breaking sports*

1) Base jumping
2) Rock climbing
3) Motorcycle racing
4) Bull riding
5) Horse riding
6) Heli-skiing
7) Rugby
8) Soccer
9) Skateboarding
10) Roller-skating

* Again, not in perfect order, but you get the idea!

What do double-jointed people look like on X-rays?

They look about the same as everybody else. 'Double joints' don't show up on X-rays, because in reality there's no such thing. With a few very rare exceptions, we all have the same number of bones and joints. It's the tendons, ligaments and cartilage that tie the joints together that look different in 'double-jointed' people.

What do you mean, there's no such thing as double joints?

It's true. Apart from a very few people (and we're talking one in a million here) with rare bone deformities, everyone has more or less the same number of bones and joints. So for the most part there's really no such thing as a 'double joint'.

Course there is. My mate Dave can bend his thumb all the way back to his forearm. And there's this girl in my PE class who can turn her elbows inside out AND put both feet behind her head. You're telling me they're not double-jointed?

Well, you can *call* those people 'double-jointed', but that doesn't mean they actually have double joints. The reason why these unusually flexible friends can bend and twist the way they do is not really to do with the shape of their bones. It's to do with the unusual length and stretchiness of their ligaments, tendons and cartilage.

What are they, then?

Ligaments are the tight little fleshy cords that tie the ends of bones together. If you have a model skeleton in your school's science or biology lab, you may have noticed that there are little metal wires holding the bones together. Without them, the whole thing would fall apart. Well, ligaments basically go where these wires are – between the bones in your skeleton.

How many bones are there in your body?

It depends how old you are. You're born with 300–350 bones, but as you grow from baby into toddler many of these fuse together. By the time you're fully grown, you end up with a total of 206 solid bones in your body. These 206 bones are then tied together with around 900 ligaments.

So there's more than one ligament per bone?

Well spotted – yes. There are more than four times as many ligaments as bones, and most joints have more than one ligament holding them together. The shoulder joint, for example, contains three major bones – the **humerus** (or upper arm bone), the **scapula** (or shoulder blade) and the **clavicle** (or collarbone). These three bones are held together by five major ligaments, plus a large number of tendons,

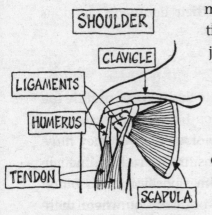

SHOULDER

CLAVICLE

LIGAMENTS

HUMERUS

TENDON

SCAPULA

muscles and bands of fibrous tissue. Ligaments stabilize joints by preventing the bones from separating too much. Unlike muscles, they're not very flexible. (Although they do stretch a little, you should think of them more like taut cables than bendy rubber bands).

Next up are the **tendons**. Like ligaments, tendons are bands of fleshy tissue that tie bones together. But they also attach muscles to bones, and they're generally a bit more stretchy than ligaments, allowing more 'give' in the joint. Tendons far outnumber ligaments in the body – there are about 4,000 of them altogether – and while each joint usually only has one or two ligaments, there are usually several tendons overlapping each other, all around the joint.

The ends of bones are covered with a thin layer of tough, plastic-like material called **cartilage**. Cartilage helps to lubricate the joints, stopping the bones from grinding against one another too much, and also helps absorb impacts along the length of the joint. If the cartilage gets torn or damaged (footballers often have this injury in their knee joints), it can be very painful, and it prevents the joint from moving freely.

So do double-jointed people have extra-long ligaments or super-stretchy tendons or something?

That's pretty much it, yes. So-called 'double-jointed' people may have unusually long ligaments that, for example, allow them to bend their fingers or thumbs back on themselves without snapping. Or they may have super-stretchy tendons in their hips, which allow them to rotate their feet backwards, or place their ankles behind their heads. And your friend with the freaky backwards elbows probably has unusually long or stretchy ligaments and tendons in his shoulder joints, which allow him to pop the humerus right out of the socket and back again. Most 'double-jointed' people also have more pliable cartilage between their joints, which can be stretched or twisted further before ripping and tearing.

So why can't you see these things on X-rays?

Because X-rays only reveal bones inside the body. Tendons, ligaments and cartilage aren't dense enough to absorb X-rays, which go straight through, leaving dark, empty patches on the X-ray plate. So unless the 'double-jointed' person shows some other sign of his/her stretchy tendons – such as an unusually wide gap between the bones of the hip or shoulder – then their secret ability will be invisible to their doctors.

Coooool. Secret stretchy people. Sounds like a superhero movie or something. So could I develop super-bendy joints by stretching my tendons or taking my cartilage out?

You can't do it all at once, no. Overstretching your tendons all at once or removing your cartilage would lead to *less* flexibility in the joints, not more (not to mention a lot of pain). But you *can* stretch tendons over time with some types of exercise like yoga. It may take months or years of practice to get super-bendy, and your tendons may never be as bendy as someone with naturally loose and flexible tendons and ligaments. But if you stick at it, you too could be impressing your friends with your freaky fingers and bendy legs. Try the exercise below to get started.

Wicked. Sign me up!

Bendy Arms

Kneel down on the floor and place your palms on the ground in front of your knees. Now keep your palms on the ground, but rotate your hands outwards until your fingers and thumbs are pointing back towards you. Inhale, then exhale as you sit back on your heels, leaving your hands in place. Your elbows should be straight and your palms pressed into the ground. Hold for thirty seconds. This will stretch and strengthen your wrists, elbows and forearms.

If exercise wears you out, how can it be good for you?

Because our bodies adapt to everything we do to them. And as far as your body is concerned, it's 'use it, or lose it'! It's not that exercise makes you healthy, it's more that a lack of exercise leaves your body weak and susceptible to disease.

Huh? That makes no sense at all.
Why's that?

Well, think about everything else in the world – like bikes, cars, computers . . . whatever. All those things wear out as you use them. Eventually the chain will snap, the engine will die or the hard drive will fail. And the more you use them the faster they wear out. Right?
Right.

So how's it any different with our bodies? I mean, shouldn't we be saving energy and using them as little as possible, so they last a bit longer?
In short, no.

Why not?
Because living bodies aren't just machines. Machines are designed and built for one main purpose. A robot arm in a car factory, for example, might be designed

to spray-paint cars at the end of the assembly line. If it's well built, it'll do its job well, and it'll keep working for a long time. But if you make it work twice as fast, or if you start using it to lift the whole car up so that other robots can put the wheels on, then the parts will quickly wear out and break down.

Living bodies, however, are different. Bodies are not just machines – they are self-building and self-repairing systems that change in response to what you use them for. When you stress the parts of your body with physical exercise, your body responds by making its parts *stronger*, not weaker.

Loading up your bones and muscles makes them stronger, thicker and tougher. Raising your heart rate and blood pressure makes your heart muscles and blood vessels larger and more powerful. Exercise also improves your ability to fight off infections from bacteria and viruses. And it even improves the function of your nervous system – giving you better reflexes, intelligence and learning abilities!

Really? Exercise even makes you cleverer?
Yep. It seems so. Biologists aren't yet certain *how* all this happens, but there's no doubt that it does. One theory is that exercise causes damage and the release of toxic chemicals in body tissues, but only in tiny amounts. These tiny toxins then trigger the body's defence and repair systems, making them stronger and better prepared to deal with damage and disease

later on. There's an old saying that 'what doesn't kill you makes you stronger'. Up to a point, biologists say, this may be true.

Okay, so what happens if you *don't* exercise?

Basically, the exact opposite. Muscles begin to waste away, becoming thinner and weaker, and bones become more brittle.* Your heart and blood vessels shrink, weaken and clog up. Your reflexes become dull, and your brain function slows. And, perhaps worst of all, your immune system weakens, leaving you vulnerable to all kinds of diseases. In fact, people who exercise are only half as likely to develop heart disease or cancer compared with people who don't. So while exercising doesn't necessarily *make* you healthy, *not* exercising leaves you seriously *un*healthy.

Yikes! So what kind of exercise should I do, and how much do I need?

Well, our caveman ancestors exercised every single day, for up to ten hours at a time! This included walking, running and climbing trees while hunting or gathering food, plus all the butchering, building and dancing that went on once they got home. That's what our bodies evolved for.

---

* This is one reason why astronauts use special exercise machines every day when they're floating about in orbit. Without exercise, their muscles and bones quickly waste away. And, even *with* exercise, most astronauts lose up to 20 per cent of their muscle and bone density by the time they return to Earth.

But the good news is that you don't need to do anywhere near that much. As long as you eat a healthy diet, just twenty to thirty minutes a day should keep you in pretty good shape, and pretty much any kind of physical exercise will do the job. Walking, running, cycling, dancing, playing sports, doing yoga, karate, kung-fu – all these things strengthen and disease-proof your body in one way or another. Plus they're great fun if you do them with your friends or family. So just pick one and get out there!

Why do we have hair on our heads, but not all over our bodies?

Actually, most of us do have hair all over our bodies. But if you're asking why we only have thick mats of hair on our heads and (ahem) other places, that's all to do with fleas, ticks, diseases and the weather.

Oh, okay. Wait . . . what? Hang on a mo – who has hair all over their body?
You do. And your mother too.

Oi! That sounds like fighting talk! Are you calling my mum a gorilla?
Goodness, no. Not at all. But while you, me and your mum may not be gorillas, we are still mammals. And, like all other mammals, human beings are *hairy*. We have hair follicles embedded in the skin, all over our bodies. In fact, apart from the palms of your hands and the soles of your feet, very few parts of your body are completely hairless.

But if that was true we'd look like we were wearing an all-over fuzzy bodysuit. I don't look like that. And neither does my mum, thank you very much.
The only reason we don't look like that is because on human skin the hairs are much thinner and less numerous than on the skin of other mammals. The

hairy coat is still there – you just can't see it so well. Hairy skin is a feature unique to mammals, which helps to keep them warm when it's cold outside while also protecting the skin from the sun when it's hotter. When it's cold, the hairs stand up and trap a layer of warm air close to the skin, insulating the body and preventing heat loss. But at the same time the hairs can also absorb or reflect direct sunlight before it reaches the skin. This prevents most mammals from getting sunburn and skin cancer, and may also protect against overheating and sunstroke. So, you see, body hair is pretty handy stuff.

But if it's *that* handy, why aren't we still all super-hairy, like cats, dogs and gorillas?
Good question. Why aren't we that hairy? What do you think?

Errr . . . I dunno. Because we don't need the fur coat any more? Because we wear clothes instead?
Okay, that's one possible explanation. And it does seem to make sense. After all, while human hairs still stand up and trap warm air when we get chilly, they're far too thin to make a huge difference if we're caught naked in a snowstorm. And now we have thermal undies and Gore-Tex ski jackets, we shouldn't need body hair any more, right?

Right.

But from what evolutionary anthropologists (scientists who study ancient and prehistoric people) tell us, humans lost their thick body hair long before they started wearing clothes. So how did they survive in the meantime?

Ah. Good point. Errr . . . warm caves? And fire?
Okay – not bad. It's true that humans are the only mammals to make fires to warm themselves and their homes. And that may well explain how humans survived without thick, hairy coats. But it still doesn't explain why they lost them in the first place. And, as far as we can figure out, that all comes down to lice.

Lice? Like head lice? Urgghhh.
Yes, lice, along with fleas, ticks and other disease-carrying parasites that like to make their homes in the hairy coats of mammals. If you think about it, you hear about head lice on people all the time. But you rarely hear about people checking you for body lice. So why is that?

Errr . . . because we don't have enough hair on our bodies for them to live in?
Exactly. And that, probably, is the reason why we humans lost our thick body hair. Humans, like other apes, are social animals who live in groups, tribes or communities. The bigger those groups are, the more likely it is that diseases and parasitic insects will

spread from person to person, making everyone ill. With less body hair, humans became less susceptible to lice. And, unlike other mammals, we could survive without our hair thanks to fires and handmade shelters. So the less-hairy humans survived better than the hairy ones and, over time, the only thick patches of hair left were on our heads, in our armpits and (ahem) in a few other places.

Okay, so why are we still hairy *there*? What's the point in just having hairy caps and pit-warmers? Well, there are a few different answers to that. Head hair and armpit hair still help prevent heat loss. And thick hair does still protect the thin scalp of a non-baldy against sunburn and sunstroke. But, on top of that, a thick head of hair is also a sign of good health (since starvation and some illness cause hair loss, suggesting the opposite – poor health). With this in mind, scientists also think that we still have head hair because human females – throughout history – have picked up on this sign, and chosen hairy-headed, healthy-looking mates over unhealthy-looking baldies almost every time.

That just leaves the armpit and the short-and-curly-nether-region hair (also known as pubic hair) that grows around your groin from puberty onwards. And this, it seems, may be down to attraction too. These hairs trap pheromones – special scented chemicals produced by sebaceous glands in the armpits and groin,* which are thought to attract members of the opposite sex.

So hairy pits are . . . smell-trappers?
Exactly.

So why do we bother washing them and using deodorant? Shouldn't we just let 'em pong, so the girls – or guys – will come running?
Well, there's a big difference between 'fresh, musky scent' and 'three-day-old cabbage-and-onion pits'. If I were you, I'd wash 'em anyway . . .

* See 'Why do sweaty feet stink?' on page 136 for more about this.

How do karate masters chop through concrete?

They simply drive the tough bones of their hands through the slab or block at high speed, aiming at just the right spot. Though you may not believe it, bones are actually much tougher than concrete. So, if it's done right, the karate-chop battle of bone-versus-block only has one winner.

Bones are tougher than concrete? No way! That's impossible!

It's true. Living bone is a far stronger material than artificial concrete. In fact, if you used a machine to snap a human leg bone, then did the same thing with a concrete cylinder of the same basic shape and weight, the leg bone could withstand over *forty times* more force before snapping.

So if my bones were made of concrete, they would break more easily?

Exactly.

But how? I thought concrete was some of the toughest stuff around. Isn't that why we build buildings and bridges out of it?

Concrete certainly is a very tough material. But it's also quite brittle, and cracks easily if bent or twisted.* This is where bone has the advantage. From the outside, bone seems like a dry, brittle material. But in fact it's more like a very thick, solid gel, with chalky minerals trapped inside. Cut a living bone open, and you'll see that the bit in the middle – the marrow – is spongy and fleshy. (This is missing from most dinosaur bones in museums, as it has long since rotted away or fossilized.)

As the bone grows, living bone cells from the marrow, called **osteocytes**, surround themselves with a criss-crossing web of protein and sugar molecules. This fleshy, fibrous web then traps water, along with calcium and phosphorus, squeezed into it by the osteocytes. Over time, the web hardens into a chalky gel, rich in calcium phosphate – the same material that clams, oysters and mussels use to build their shells.

So we're a bit like shellfish, only we build our shells on the inside?
You could say that, yes. Anyway, what you end up with is a very tough, strong material which is also very lightweight. Better still, because of its partly fleshy, watery structure, bone isn't brittle like concrete. In many ways, it's the ideal building material. If we could build houses and bridges out of it, we probably

---

* For this reason, solid concrete sections of bridges and buildings are reinforced with steel rods. If they weren't, they could easily be damaged or destroyed by high winds or earth tremors.

would. (Who knows – someday, maybe we will!) Try to bend, twist or crush a piece of bone and it will bend quite a bit before it cracks. This allows bone to absorb far more force and impact than a similar weight of concrete. If you want to see for yourself just how bendy bones can be, try the experiment on page 173.

Is that why a bony hand can chop through a concrete block?

Partly, yes. The bones in your hand are many times stronger than wooden boards, clay tiles, or even concrete blocks. Plus your hand-bones are reinforced with a covering of muscles, tendons, cartilage and skin. As a solid lump of flesh, your hand could easily slap through a concrete block if you hit it hard enough.

So could *I* chop a block in half like a karate master?

In theory, yes. Anyone with healthy bones could do it. But without the proper training I wouldn't try it.

Why's that?

Because karate masters take no chances. They spend months or years toughening up the skin of their hands by hitting wooden posts wrapped in string, or boards covered in foam. Over time, the skin on their hands responds by thickening into a tough, fibrous callus over the knuckles or edge of the hand.

170

They also practise hitting the boards, blocks or tiles with enough speed. Your hand is tough, but without enough speed and momentum it would just bounce off (quite painfully and embarassingly). So masters practise with thin wooden boards before having a crack at concrete or tiles.

Where and *how* you hit the block is also very important, and it takes practice to get it right. Karate masters often focus more force on the block by hitting it with a small surface area – like the first two knuckles of the fist or the blade-like edge of the hand – rather than the whole palm. And they aim right for the centre of the board, tile or block. This is the weakest point of the object, as it's furthest from the propped-up edges, giving them more leverage as they strike.

What about when they break whole stacks of things? I've seen 'em do that too. Could I do that?
Yes, you could. When karate-choppers break whole stacks of blocks or tiles, you may notice that they create a gap between them by putting a pair of sticks at the edges of each one. That way, if they can generate enough force to blast through the top one, the impact gets transferred to the weakest point of the next – and so on, all the way to the bottom of the pile. But again – you need training and practice.

What if I took some tiles out of my dad's shed, piled 'em up and had a go at it right now? What would happen then?
You'd probably break a finger or cut your hand. And all your friends would laugh.

Oh. I guess I shouldn't try that, then.
No. You shouldn't. Trust me, there are easier – and far less painful – ways to impress your mates.

Experiment: bendy bones

As hard and chalky as they seem, it's hard to imagine that our bones are actually quite flexible, and made mostly of water. If you want to see for yourself, just try this experiment with a chicken bone from the butcher's . . .

1) Get a leftover wing bone or wishbone from the butcher, and ask him (or a helpful parent) to clean off all the flesh, muscles and tendons. Then leave it overnight to dry. (Be sure to hide it from your cat or dog, or they'll make off with it and ruin the progress of science!)
2) Try bending it between your fingers. It probably won't bend much, but have a go. Don't break it, though!
3) Grab a bottle of vinegar, and a glass jar with a tight-fitting lid. Put the bone in the jar, and fill it with enough vinegar to cover it completely.
4) Screw the lid on, and leave it alone for one full week.
5) Unscrew the jar, pour out the vinegar remove the bone, and rinse it with water.
6) Try bending the bone between your fingers, as you did before. What happens?

(See page 235 for the answer, and why this works.)

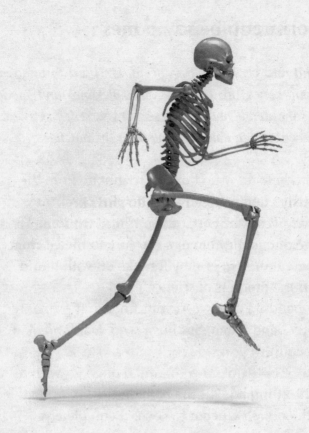

Do old people shrink as they age?

Yes and no. Many people do get shorter as they age. But, when they do, it isn't because they're shrinking all over. They simply lose height as their spine becomes shorter and more curved due to disuse, disease and the effects of gravity.

Seriously? Old people really do shrink?

In a way, yes. Many (but not all) men and women do lose height as they get older. Men lose an average of 3–4 cm (1.5 in) in height as they age, while women may lose 5 cm (2 in) or more.

So if you live to be 200 years old – would you keep shrinking till you were, like, 60 cm tall? Like a little baby again?

No, you wouldn't.

Why not?

Because old people don't really *shrink*. It's not that they're growing in reverse – their legs, arms and backbones getting shorter until they end up like toddlers or leprechauns. When they do get shorter, it's because the spine has shortened a little. Or, more often, become more bent and curved.

So the bones don't shrink at all?

Well, bones can and do shrink and thin out as you

get older. As you may know, bones don't just stop growing once you reach adulthood. They're being worn down, regrown and reshaped throughout your whole lifetime. As you get older, the ingredients (or composition) of your bones changes. Old bone tissue is still being broken down, but gaps appear where new tissue fails to grow. Over time, this leaves bones more weak and brittle, which is why many older people may break their hips, wrists and other bones when they take even a gentle tumble. Certain diseases like **osteoporosis** (which means 'bone hole disease') speed up this process, and can leave sufferers with weak, brittle bones even at a fairly young age.

So is that what happens to the spine? It gets gaps in it and crumbles?

Not really, no. While the bones of the spine may lose a little mass over your lifetime, it's not the bones themselves, but the spaces between them that shrink as you get older. Squashed between each bone (or **vertebra**) is a disc of gel-like cartilage, which sits in the intervertebral space and lubricates the twisting and bending movements of the spine. This keeps the spine moving freely and easily and prevents the vertebrae from grinding against each other and wearing down – much as engine oil prevents engine parts wearing down in a car. Over time, the constant downward pull of gravity squashes these discs flatter, making the spaces between the vertebrae smaller and the whole spine shorter. This is part of what makes older people seem to shrink as they age.

So when does this all start? When you're forty? Fifty? Sixty?

As a matter of fact, it's happening to you already. When you go to bed tonight, you'll probably be about half an inch (1 cm) shorter than you were this morning.

***What?* Really?**

Yep. Every day, your spine is squashed and shortened as you move about upright. And each night, your spine lengthens out again as you flatten yourself out to sleep. So, if you're measuring yourself to see how tall you are, do it first thing in the morning, as you'll be shorter by tonight!

Yagggghhh! But I don't want to shrink! It's not fair! I haven't stopped growing yet!

Don't worry – no need to panic. That's not the whole story. (And there's good news at the end of it.)

While the daily compression (or squashing) of your spine does cause you to get temporarily shorter, it bounces back each day, and it takes an entire lifetime before you permanently lose even a centimetre of height this way. Most of the 'shortening' we see in old people as they age isn't shrinking or shortening at all – it's bending.

Everyone has a slight 'S'-shaped bend to their spine. Even young people. You need this shape to absorb the shock of walking, running, jumping and lifting. If your spine was completely straight, like a pillar or column, it would be too easily damaged and injured by stresses and impacts. The S-shape allows your spine to act like a coiled spring, flexing and bouncing back as you load it up with weight or send shockwaves into it with a heavy landing.

But if you're not careful – and you don't sit, stand and walk correctly – the bend in your spine can widen out into a real S-shape. This leaves your head jutting forward on your neck, your back hunched, your hips jutting out backwards, and your knees bent painfully beneath your body. Once you reach this state, you can no longer straighten up to your full height, and you're forced to take small, shuffling steps when you walk.

So that's why old people walk all bent over like that?

Right. But the *good* news is: not *all* old people suffer this fate and, if you do the right things, you won't have to either. If you're careful to sit up straight, and avoid slouching when you walk, it will help you keep your spine straight well into old age. And certain types of exercise – like yoga, Pilates, dance and martial arts – can help you straighten yourself out permanently, and keep a straight, supple spine for life. If you're as careful with your spine as you are with your teeth, both will stay in good nick even when you're old and wrinkly. Keep your spine in good shape, and you could still be running marathons, doing tai chi and dancing when you're 105!

Sounds good to me. Where do I start?
Have a go at the exercises below. Do these every day, and you'll be standing tall in no time. Then teach them to your mum, your dad, your grandma or grandad. Who knows – they might get taller too!

Keep Your Spine in Shape

1) Lie on your back with feet flat. Inhale, arch your back and press the tip of your coccyx (or tailbone) hard into the floor. As you exhale, flatten yourself out again and press your lower back hard into the ground. Repeat slowly ten times.
2) Lie on your belly and turn your face to the left and place the back of your left hand beneath your cheek like a pillow. Now inhale and lift your left hand, elbow and head off the ground, looking over your left shoulder at your feet behind you. At the same time, lift your right leg off the ground – keeping it straight and lifting it from the hip. Now exhale, lowering your leg, hand, elbow and head, then switch sides.
3) Do this every day for a strong, healthy spine!

Why do we have toes?

The simple answer is we inherited our toes from our tree-dwelling animal ancestors, who used them to climb, dangle and swing on branches. Later on, as two-legged humans, we kept them because they proved useful for walking, running and leaping.

You mean we inherited them from monkeys?

Not quite. We didn't actually evolve from monkeys. But our ape-like ancestors did have gripping (or prehensile) feet, which they used to grip tree branches just as modern-day monkeys do. And, in fact, we can trace our toes a lot further back than that. Long before our animal ancestors evolved into apes, they were little shrew-like mammals with four paws and five toes on each. Before that, they were four-legged, five-toed reptiles. And, before *that*, four-legged amphibians, much like big newts.

So all animals have five toes on each foot?

With a few exceptions, yes. Fish, of course, never had toes in the first place. And invertebrates (animals without backbones) like insects, crabs and squid have very different body structures to vertebrates (or animals with backbones). So they don't count here.

Among the vertebrates, some animals (like snakes and whales) had feet and toes once, but have since lost them altogether, while others (like horses) stand on enlarged middle toes (the other toes shrivelled up and reduced beside them). But the vast majority of mammals, birds, reptiles and amphibians have five toes on each foot. So, like them, we have five toes.

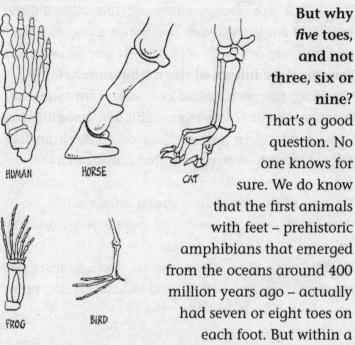

HUMAN   HORSE   CAT

FROG   BIRD

But why *five* toes, and not three, six or nine? That's a good question. No one knows for sure. We do know that the first animals with feet – prehistoric amphibians that emerged from the oceans around 400 million years ago – actually had seven or eight toes on each foot. But within a few million years five-toed land animals started to become more common, and seven and eight-toed animals began to die off. For some reason, five turned out to be the ideal number of feety digits. And since most of today's vertebrate land animals (including us) evolved from those five-toed pioneers, most of them (or, rather, *us*) have five toes too.

Okay, so I understand how bendy, finger-like toes would've come in handy for tree-swinging monkey-and-lemur-type things. But what good did they do us once we came down from the trees?

When our ape-like ancestors left the safety of the trees and started walking upright on the plains and savannahs of Africa, their toes got shorter and stubbier over time, so that they were no longer much use for climbing. But, as it turned out, stubby toes were still quite handy for balancing upright on two feet. So, as early and modern humans evolved, we kept our toes to help us with walking, running and jumping.

Do toes really make that much difference?

Absolutely. You can see for yourself if you want. Try this:

Take your shoes off, and stand upright on a flat surface. Now lift one foot, and balance on the other for a minute or more. What happens?

Errr . . . I wobble about a bit. And I nearly fall over, a few times.

Right. Now do it again, but this time lift all the toes on your supporting foot off the ground. What happens now?

Okay . . . I fell over pretty quickly that time.

Right. Now go back to the first experiment, and try

to feel what your toes are doing. Feel the tension in the muscles of your toes come and go as you wobble to and fro.

While you may not always notice it, your toes are constantly making tiny adjustments (called **micro-adjustments**) to your balance while you're standing. These little pushes from your toes keep your centre of balance (in this case, your hips) above your feet, stopping you from toppling forward or backwards. As you stand, your big toes alone bear around a quarter of your total weight.

So without toes it would be far more difficult to maintain your balance on one foot, or to shift your balance easily from one foot to the other while walking and running. Try walking or running with your toes pulled up, and you'll see what I mean – you'll probably look more like a clumsy chicken than an Olympic athlete!

[Trip, crash!] Ow!
See what I mean?

Okay, okay. I get it. But answer me this. If toes are so great (ouch!), how come it hurts so much when you stub one on a chair?
Because your toes need lots of sensory nerves in order to sense the shape and slope of the ground beneath them. This allows you to walk over almost any terrain without constantly looking down. But, unfortunately,

alongside these touch-sensitive toe-nerves is another set of nerves that sense pain. *These* are there to stop you whacking your toes into things too hard and damaging the delicate sensory nerves and tissues inside. So when you stub your toe on something they really let you know it! Best thing you can do is rub and squeeze, to help soften the pain with more touch.

Yowch! That totally sucks, dude.
Toe-tally?

Oh, very funny. Grrrrrr . . .

Why do your fingers go wrinkly in the bath?

Because your skin is actually an organ system made up of separate layers of tissue. Spend too long in the bath, and the dry outer layer will expand and spread out while the layer beneath stays put. This creates folds and wrinkles in spots where your skin is especially tight – like your feet, hands and fingertips.

Wait – skin is an organ?
Yes, it is. In fact, it's the largest organ in the body.

But I thought organs were, y'know, like big lumps of meaty stuff . . .
Well, an organ is just a collection of tissues that work together for a common purpose. And while most organs are a bit easier to play football with, that doesn't mean your skin doesn't qualify. Skin isn't just a flat, boring sheet of body tissue. It's actually very complex. It's made up of two separate tissue layers – called the **dermis** and **epidermis** – and also contains other tissues like hair, nails, glands and nerve endings.

The **dermis** (which is just Latin for 'skin') is a rich, living layer of skin cells, blood vessels, sweat glands and oil glands. This is the pink, bloody bit that gets exposed if you manage to graze or chop off more than a few millimetres of skin in an accident. But ordinarily you never see it because above (or outside) this lies the epidermis.

The **epidermis** (which means 'outer skin') itself contains two layers – an outer layer of hard, dry, dead skin cells that are constantly shed from the body, and an underlying layer of living skin cells that grow, divide and push upwards to replace the ones you've shed.

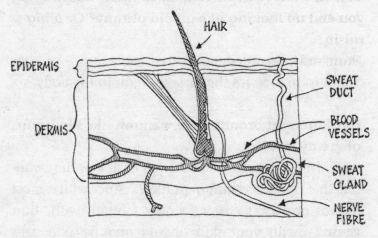

It's the *outer* part of the epidermis that goes wrinkly in the bath. This is because the cells in the under-layer are firmly attached to each other and to the dermis beneath. But the cells in the outer layer are not. So when your warm bath water is absorbed into the dry, outer layer of the epidermis, it swells up, spreads out, and forms ripples and wrinkles.

But why doesn't that happen all the time – like every time you wash your hands?

Because ordinarily your epidermis is kept oily and waterproof by oil glands in the dermis. But if you spend too long underwater (and especially in warm water) the oil gets washed out and water begins to seep in. The longer you stay in the bath, the more water is absorbed and the wrinklier you get.

So if you stayed in there long enough, would you end up looking like an old granny? Or a big raisin?
Thankfully, no. There's only so much water your skin can absorb, so there's a limit to how wrinkly you get.

That's a relief. So is that what skin is for, then? To keep water out?
Actually, it's designed to keep water in, rather than out. Since your body is 60–75 per cent water, it has to keep as much of it in as possible, only allowing out small amounts through sweat, tears and urine. So the tough, oily barrier of your skin helps prevent your body from dehydrating. And, as an organ system, skin does loads of other useful jobs within the body.

Like what?
Well, it's not just a barrier to water. It also forms a fleshy shield against bacteria, viruses and other nasty microbes. It protects our bodies from harmful chemicals and radiation. It stores fat and water, which help to insulate the body against extreme

temperatures. And it helps to control our inner body temperature, using hairs and sweat glands to trap and release heat.

Wow! Skin is pretty clever stuff.

That's not all! Skin is also a huge sense organ, and without it you'd have serious trouble figuring out what the world around you was up to. Nerve endings embedded in your skin sense temperature, pressure and pain, and work together to give you your sense of touch. Without it, you'd have serious trouble walking and picking things up, let alone running, dancing, writing, drawing or playing video games. And, believe it or not, skin even helps with digestion and nutrition.

What? How?

For starters, your skin uses sunlight to produce vitamin D, which helps you to absorb nutrients. It helps you get rid of things too. While body wastes and toxic chemicals are mostly peed and pooed out of your body, they're also sweated out through your skin.

Your skin can even absorb some vitamins and medicines that help to keep you healthy. Ever seen those medicine 'patches' you slap on your arm? Well, it's through capillaries (tiny blood vessels) in the skin that these drugs and medicines are taken into the bloodstream. In the future, more and more of our medicines may be delivered this way rather than in pills and injections.

But you can't actually *eat* through your skin, right?
Right. Sadly, most food particles are too large to get through. And, even if you could absorb food through your skin, your immune cells would probably just attack the undigested food blobs once they made it into your bloodstream, thinking they were dangerous bacteria. So, while slapping on the beef stew like suntan lotion might be fun, it won't do you much good.

It may, however, make you very popular with your dog . . .

6. Grey Matters

Why does it feel weird when you step on to a stationary escalator?
Because your brain stores memories of how to keep your balance on a moving escalator, and goes on to 'escalator autopilot' just as you're about to step on. When it discovers the steps aren't moving, it takes a while for the autopilot to switch off, leaving you very surprised and confused!

My brain has an autopilot?
Sort of, yes.

Sweet! So can I switch it on in the mornings, and it'll get me out of bed and off to school while I just chill out? I guess I could wake up and take over my body around 10, maybe . . .
Hang on, that's not . . .

. . . On second thoughts, why stop there? Why not just leave the autopilot on through all the boring classes, and only take over for the fun ones, like Art and PE . . .
Wait, wait, wait! Hold up there. It doesn't work like that, I'm afraid.

It doesn't? Booo. Not fair. So you were just winding me up?

No, I wasn't. The brain really does have a kind of 'autopilot' function, which can take over your movements and help you do things you've done before without concentrating too much. But that doesn't mean you can 'check out' entirely . . .

If you think about it, your brain has to have an 'autopilot', otherwise you'd have to learn complex movements – like riding a bike – over and over again. Or, at the very least, you'd have to concentrate so hard on staying on the bike that it'd be almost impossible to do anything else at the same time – like chat with friends, or listen to an MP3 player.

Hmmm. Never thought of that. So how *does* it work, then?

When you start to learn a new, complex movement skill – like walking, running or riding a bike – for a while you have to concentrate hard as you learn to balance your shifting weight and coordinate the movements of your arms and legs. The movements are made using the brain's **motor cortex** – tiny parts of which control every individual bit of the body. But the *order* or *sequence* of walking, running or riding movements is controlled by a region at the back of the brain, called the **cerebellum.**

Eventually, after many hours of practice, the whole shape and sequence of each activity becomes

MOTOR CORTEX

CEREBELLUM

permanently embedded in the cerebellum, as a kind of 'muscle memory'. After that, you no longer need to think about how to walk, run or ride again. As soon as you start stepping, running or pedalling, the 'autopilot' function in your cerebellum kicks in, and you just *do it*, without thinking. Ever heard the expression 'It's just like riding a bike – you never forget'? Well – that's why.

But what does that have to do with riding escalators? I mean, that's not exactly a *skill*, is it? You just step on and stand there.

Ah, but that's where you're wrong. Riding escalators *is* a skill – not a very impressive one, I admit, but still a skill. If you don't believe me, next time you head out to a multi-storey shopping centre or mall, take a seat near the escalator and wait for a toddler to come along. Then watch as the child tries to step on to it, leans back and almost falls over.*

The only reason *you* don't do this is because you've learned the skill of escalator-riding, and your autopilot takes over. Just as you learned to balance yourself automatically on a bike, you learned a little about how to mount, ride and dismount escalators the first few times you did it. You learned to lean forward and speed up your walking pace as you got on. You learned to keep leaning forward a little (or grab the moving handrail)** to compensate for the forward motion and avoid toppling back down the steps. And you learned to take a long, striding step off the thing to avoid tripping up at the end of it.

Now, of course, all these movements are so automatic that you hardly have to think about them. That's because – like bike-riding – escalator-riding is stored permanently in your cerebellum. So, every time you approach an escalator, the autopilot kicks in and your brain starts to adjust your body to the steps automatically. Unfortunately, this still happens even when the escalator is broken, turning it – effectively – into *stairs*.

---

* Don't worry – usually they're saved from falling by a parent tugging upwards on an outstretched hand.

** Why do these things never move at quite the same speed as the steps on escalators? My hand always ends up travelling faster than me. That's a question for the engineers, I suppose . . .

So then what happens?

Exactly what you'd expect. The brain preps your body for *moving* steps, making you lean forward and speed up your stride. But since the steps *aren't* actually moving this makes it feel as if you're being 'sucked into' the escalator. (This may be the root of the common fear that, if you don't get off in time, you'll be sucked down the hole at the end along with the moving steps. Ever felt that way?)

But can't it *tell* the steps aren't moving? I thought the brain was supposed to be clever . . .

Eventually, yes – the brain *can* tell. In fact, if you ride the same broken escalator twice, it most likely won't happen the second time, as your brain has figured it out. But the first time you approach a broken escalator, even though you can see it's not moving – the memory of 'how to ride an escalator' is so strong that it overrides your conscious knowledge that you are, in fact, approaching a flight of stairs. The effect is strongest when you walk straight off a working escalator and on to a broken (and stationary) one. Try it – it'll seriously freak you out.

I will. But I think I'll get my friends to do it first.

Get it sorted: motor memory weirdness

Broken escalators aren't the only things out there that generate weird movement sensations. Ever felt weird on one of these?

Moving walkways at airports

Similar to escalators. You learn to get on, ride them and get off on autopilot. But when they're out of order, if feels like you're sucked on to them and then wading through mud.

Ships and boats

After a good stretch of time bobbing around at sea, your brain adjusts your balance automatically to compensate for the rocking motion of the deck. But when you first step off on to solid land you feel like you're still rocking and swaying.

Trampolines/bouncy castles

Bounce around for long enough and your brain starts to get the hang of it – bending and straightening your knees as your feet hit the canvas to keep your jumps high and light. But when you step off again your knees bend as you hit the solid, un-bouncy ground, and it feels like your legs weigh a ton!

Why does spinning make you dizzy?

*Because your brain gets confused between what you're seeing and what you're feeling. The brain senses that you're spinning using special gravity-and-motion-sensing organs in your inner ear, which work together with your eyes to keep your vision and balance stable. But when you suddenly **stop** spinning the system goes haywire, and your brain thinks you're moving while you're not!*

I have gravity and motion sensors in my ears? Coooooool. Why has no one told me that before?
Of course you do. How else could you know if you were moving, spinning or standing on your head, even with your eyes closed?

Hmmm. I hadn't thought about it like that. I always thought we just figured all that out by looking.
Well, of course vision plays a part in balance and movement too. (If you don't believe me, try standing on one leg for a minute with your eyes open, and then with your eyes closed.) But your brain receives input and information from both eyes and ears in order to figure out which way up you are, how you're currently moving and whether you're moving at all.

So what do these motion sensors look like? If you look in your ear, can you see them?

Errr . . . how would you go about looking in your own ear?

All right, then – someone else's ear.

Well, you still wouldn't be able to see much. Your organs of balance and motion – called the **vestibular organs** – are behind the eardrum, deep within the inner ear. They sit behind the snail-like hearing organ called the **cochlea**, just behind a cavity called the **vestibule**,* from which the organs get their name.

Each organ features three **semicircular canals** – three little loops or tubes that sit at different angles to each other so that they can sense both horizontal and vertical movements of the head. The inside of each canal is filled with a gloopy fluid called **endolymph** and lined with thousands of tiny hairs called **cilia**.

Now, here's the clever bit. The base of each hair is attached to a tiny branch of the vestibular nerve, which leads back to the brain. Every time you move, rotate or tilt your head, the gloopy

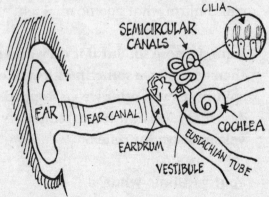

* This means 'entrance hall' in Latin.

endolymph liquid swishes within the semicircular canals, bending the cilia over like bits of seaweed in an ocean tide. Once bent, these little hairs send a signal to the brain, telling it how fast (and in what direction) your head is moving.

Together with a set of little gravity-sensing structures called **otoliths** (which sit just beside the semicircular canals), your vestibular organs can sense any type and direction of motion, and relay that information to the brain so that it can figure out:

a) your *orientation*, or which way up your body is, relative to the ground

b) your *linear acceleration*, or how fast you're moving in a given direction, and

c) your *angular acceleration*, or how fast and in which direction you're rotating or spinning

. . . and all this works even with your eyes closed. Your eyes just supply extra information, so that your brain can confirm what's going on. Pretty neat, eh?

Yeah, I s'pose so. But if it all works so well, then why do we sometimes feel like we're still spinning, even after we've stopped?
Ah, that's because of a temporary upset in your **vestibulo-ocular reflex**.

Your vestibulo-what?
The **vestibulo-ocular** (or **V-O**) **reflex** stabilizes your vision while you're moving or spinning. Basically,

it stops the world going blurry as it whizzes by in the opposite direction. It does this by sending information* about how you're moving from the vestibular organs in the ears to the muscles that move the eyes. When your eye muscles receive this info, they respond by rotating (or rather, making lots of little rotating movements) in the opposite direction to the way you're spinning. That way, your eyes can keep 'scanning' or 'scrolling' your surroundings, keeping them in focus even as they whizz past you.

This all works fine until you come to a sudden stop. When you stop spinning suddenly, your head and body stop moving, but the fluid in your semicircular canals keeps sloshing around, and it takes a while for the bent-over cilia to right themselves and stop sending 'I'm spinning' signals to the eye muscles. So the eyes just do what they're told, and they keep scrolling backwards to compensate for the spin. This makes it seem as if the whole world is still wheeling around you (in the opposite direction to the way you were just spinning), even though you're standing or sitting quite still!

Whoa. Crazy. But then why does that make you fall over or feel sick?
If you're standing or sitting straight, with your head

---

* Through nerves, of course. It wouldn't do much good if they had to telephone or email your eyeballs instead, would it?

vertical and upright, it doesn't. Within ten to twenty seconds your brain figures out what's going on, the spinning sensation stops, and you're fine. But if you tilt your head off-centre – by leaning backwards, forward or off to one side – *that's* when the problems start.

Assuming you're spinning off-centre like an out-of-control figure skater, your brain attempts to correct your posture – shifting the alignment of your knees, hips and spine to bring you upright again. But since you're *not actually spinning at all* this does no good whatsoever! Instead, it makes you lean and teeter off balance and (very probably) fall to the ground in a confused heap. Also, the mismatch between the info your brain is getting from the ears and what it can see with your eyes may cause **motion sickness**, which is what makes you feel queasy and ill.

Want to try it for yourself? Have a go at the movement and balance experiments opposite, and have fun fooling your eyes, ears and brain! (Just be careful, and don't throw up on the carpet.)

Experiment: you spin me (right round)

Ready to dizzy it up for yourself? Take care, stay safe and don't do these so long that you make yourself sick. But give them a quick try, and feel for yourself how your balance organs work.

1) Grab a short stick, put one end to the ground, and run in a circle round that point ten to twelve times. Now stop quickly, drop the stick and try to walk in a straight line. How'd it go?
2) Now sit on a swivelling chair and get a friend to spin you round quickly, ten to twelve times, then stop you suddenly. How does that feel? Any different?
3) Now repeat the experiment above, but close your eyes. Open them once you stop. How was that? Room still spinning, or not?
4) Finally, repeat the experiment once more, this time with your head tilted *slightly* to one side during the spin. Feel better or worse? Read through the previous chapter again, and see if you can figure out what's happening in your ears, eyes and brain to make you dizzy.

Where do feelings and emotions come from?

Mostly from an ancient part of the brain called the **limbic system***. All mammals have this brain region – from mice and shrews to cats, dogs, chimps and humans. So all mammals feel basic emotions like fear, pain and pleasure. But since human feelings also involve other, newer bits of the brain, we feel more complex emotions than any other animal on the planet.*

So feelings aren't just kept in one spot and released into the brain from there?

No, not quite. Although some emotions may originate in specific parts of the brain, there's no single 'happy spot' or 'angry spot'. Instead, emotions like happiness and anger are formed through the interaction of many different spots, across different regions and layers of the brain. In general, the more *primitive* (or 'animalistic') *emotions* – like fear, rage and disgust – come from *older* regions of the brain, found deeper down inside. Meanwhile, the *higher emotions* like hope, compassion and regret come from newer brain regions[*] closer to the surface. But, in practice, human emotions usually involve *many* regions of the brain – both old and new – working together to create a single feeling.

---

[*] Most other mammals do not feel these emotions, because their brains lack the newer, outer brain regions needed to generate them.

So some bits of my brain are older than others?
In terms of evolution, yes.

I don't get it. I mean, I was born with my brain, right. So if *I'm* eight years old, my *brain* is eight years old too!
That's true. But the brain you've inherited from your animals ancestors wasn't all formed at the same time. Different parts developed at different points in evolutionary history, and the older bits are millions of years older than the newest ones.

Look at it this way – in the history of evolution, fish evolved backbones before they evolved legs and became amphibians. After *that,* it was millions of years before some of their mammalian descendants evolved hands with thumbs. So, in evolutionary terms, thumbs came after legs, which came after backbones. Just because you now enjoy the benefits of all these things, and were born with the full set, that doesn't mean they all developed at the same point in history.

And that's how it is with the layers of your brain?
Exactly. You can divide the brain into three basic layers. The oldest and deepest is the **brainstem**, which is essentially the top end of your spinal cord plus a small bulge that sits on top. Wrapped around that, like a fleshy peach around its stone, is the second-oldest brain region, which contains the **limbic**

system. Outside that is the brain's newest region, the **neocortex**. The name, in Latin, means 'new shell'. And that's pretty much what it looks like – a thick, wrinkly nutshell that covers the inner regions of the brain. This region is only fully developed in humans and other higher mammals.

Historically, the three layers developed from the inside out. They also develop this way in a human embryo – with the brainstem growing first, followed by the limbic system and finally the neocortex.

So what does each bit do?

The **brainstem** is responsible for creating the most primitive **emotional reactions or reflexes**. These include **fear** or **aggression** in response to pain, and **happiness** (or **relief**) at finding safety or food. Even reptile and amphibian brains contain this most ancient region. So, as you might expect, snakes, lizards, frogs and newts all show these emotional reactions. It's sometimes nicknamed 'the dinosaur brain' for this reason.

The **limbic system** contains several different brain regions, each with its own role in creating emotions. This is where most of our **basic emotions** come from. It includes:

The **Amygdala** – This controls **fear**, **rage** and **aggression**. Damage to this brain region in animals makes them completely fearless. In humans, it leaves them unable to decide whether they like or dislike somebody.

The **Hippocampus** – This is involved in the formation of **learned emotions** or **emotional memories**. If this region is damaged, you can't retain any new memories at all. So even if you were terrified by a snake attack once before, without a working hippocampus, you wouldn't remember what it felt like (so wouldn't be afraid of snakes) the next time you encountered one.

The **Thalamus** and **Hypothalamus** – These regions create **desires** that help you to regulate the body, such as hunger and thirst. If you get too hot or cold, these regions create the desire to seek shade or shelter. If you or your family are attacked, they create the desire to fight back.

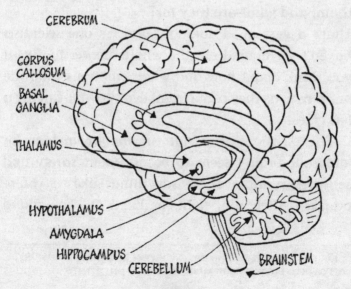

CEREBRUM

CORPUS CALLOSUM

BASAL GANGLIA

THALAMUS

HYPOTHALAMUS

AMYGDALA

HIPPOCAMPUS

CEREBELLUM

BRAINSTEM

Finally, outside the brainstem and limbic system, the neocortex helps create more complex human emotions like **hope**, **joy**, **love**, **sadness**, **disgust** and **despair**. This region of the brain is only fully developed in humans. So while other intelligent mammals may also experience these emotions, they don't feel them the same way we do.

I don't know about that. Our dog *loves* everybody. And our cat looks pretty *disgusted* when you give her the wrong brand of cat food . . .
Like I said, it all depends how intelligent your mammal is. Get yourself a pet chimp or dolphin,* and you'd see an even wider range of emotions.

So what's the point in emotions? Why do we have them, and what are they for?
That's a very good question, and it's one scientists haven't yet figured out the whole answer to. But if you think about how and when emotions (and the brain regions they came from) evolved you can get a few clues.

The emotions that start in the **brainstem** (or 'dinosaur brain') seem to be all about **safety** and **self-preservation**. These say things like 'If you're attacked, then run, fight, or bite,' or, 'You found

---

* I'm not really suggesting this. Neither of these animals should be kept as pets. But you know what I mean.

food – that's good – be happy.'

The emotions that come from the **limbic system** (or 'mammalian brain') are also about survival, and interact with the brainstem to create fear, anger, aggression, hunger and thirst – all of which help to keep animals safe. But they're also about **communication** and getting along with other animals in a pack or group. The limbic system helps you express emotions like pleasure, happiness, fear and anger so that you can let others know what you're feeling.

Finally, the higher emotions of the **neocortex** allow humans (and a few other social, intelligent animals) to **communicate with** and **understand each other** in more complex, 'human' ways. Expressions of joy, love, hope, despair and disgust are all signals that help us to look after each other and work together in more sophisticated ways than other animals.

But while humans do have these higher emotions and brain regions, it's worth remembering that we still have the older, more primitive ones too. When you're truly scared, your 'dinosaur brain' will override the higher emotions, and you'll run, fight and do anything to stay alive. Even hunger and thirst can make you forget other people as your limbic system drives your fierce desire to find food and water.

Wow. With all those emotions, it's a wonder we ever get anything done at all!
Well, we humans also have the unique ability to

understand and control our emotions, which helps! That said, just because we *can* control our 'animal emotions', that doesn't mean we all *do*. Sadly, the world is still full of people who give in to their hunger,

desire, fear, anger and rage – people who cheat, steal, fight and kill like reptiles, as if they'd never evolved human brains at all.

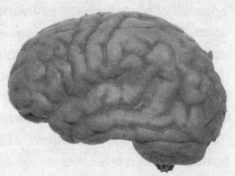

Hmmm. I guess we do. Sad, really.
But I like to think that for every cruel or criminal act driven by greed and anger, there's a positive one driven by hope, love and the desire to make each other happy. From these emotions, humans have risen above the other animals and created art, philosophy, engineering and – of course – science!

So maybe we're not so bad after all . . .

Could you live with half a brain?

Yes, you could! Your brain is divided into two halves that mirror each other in shape, size and function. And while each half does have its specialities, you could survive and learn to use just one half if the other was damaged or removed.

Your brain really has two halves? Like, you could fit your fingers in between them?

Yes, it really does. The two halves (or hemispheres) of the brain sit together in the skull, and are tethered by a cluster of nerves and blood vessels called the **corpus callosum**. Even with this holding the hemispheres together, the gap between them is big enough to slip your fingers into once the brain is outside the body (trust me – I've done it). And it's extremely easy to snip through these fleshy tethers and fold the hemisphere apart like two halves of an apple.*

But why would the brain come in two bits? Why not just one big lump of stuff – like your heart or your liver?

Because human bodies – like those of fish, birds, reptiles and most other animals – are largely symmetrical. This means that you could chop a human body in

---

* Actually, it looks a lot more like a cauliflower. And it's about the same size and weight as a bunch of bananas. But you get the idea.

half lengthways, and the left half would be a mirror image (more or less) of the right half. This is because of the way our bodies grow and develop.

On the journey from egg to embryo, we start out as a single egg. This turns into a ball of cells, which in turn lengthens out to become a flattened tube – with a head (or mouth) end, tail (or bottom) end, a front, a back, a left side and a right side. Later, as the limbs and organs develop within this body, every limb or organ (with very few exceptions) that appears on the left side is mirrored by an identical one on the right.

This is why you have two arms, two legs, two eyes, two ears and two nostrils. And, of course, these paired organs aren't just limited to the ones you can see on the outside. Inside the body, you have two lungs, two kidneys and two ovaries (if you're a girl) or two testicles (if you're a boy).

But what about your mouth, your bottom, your heart and your liver? You don't have two of those, do you?

You only have *one* mouth and *one* bottom because these form at opposite ends of the embryo while it's still a tube – *before* the embryo develops left and right 'sides'. (If they formed later, you might end up with two bottoms. Just think how weird that would be.) Other digestive organs, like the liver, pancreas, appendix, small intestine and large intestine, form as offshoots of this 'mouth-to-bottom' tube. So they don't obey the left/right rule either. And while the heart *does* end up sitting slightly to one side of the centre of the chest, it actually forms in two halves – the left and right **ventricles** – separated by a septum in the middle. And, although the left one is a little bigger, we can say that the basic structure of the heart is symmetrical too.

And that's how it is with the brain. Like the heart, it isn't quite symmetrical, and the two halves don't work independently – they work together to order information from sensory nerves, and to produce thoughts, speech and movement via motor nerves. But in a way, the two hemispheres of the brain are like your lungs, your kidneys or the other 'paired' organs in the body. Because if you lose or damage one of them, the other can take up the slack and keep you alive.

Seriously? I mean, I guess I've heard of someone losing a kidney or lung and surviving. But living with half your brain?

Yep. It's rare, but it happens. If you lose[*] or damage a kidney, the other one grows by up to 50 per cent in order to take on the extra work of filtering your blood. If you lose or damage a lung, there's little room for the remaining lung to grow, but if it's healthy it'll do its job well enough for you to survive. And in some rare cases people with brain conditions such as epilepsy have to have the connection between the two halves of their brain severed, or have an entire half of the brain removed altogether.

When this happens, fluid fills the space left behind, and it may leave the patient temporarily unable to speak or move properly. But within a year the speaking and moving functions previously handled by the missing half are taken over by the half that remains. And, believe it or not, this works well enough for the patient to live a full lifetime (although they might still suffer with some physical or mental disabilities) with – literally – half a brain.

But if you can survive with only half a brain, what do you need the other half for?

Well, while the two halves of the brain are similar, and can take over from each other if need be, they're not identical. Each half specializes in certain types of task.

---

[*]   Actually, a good number of people are born with just one kidney in the first place, due to birth defects. But, because the remaining one does its job so well, they may never know they have just one until they're X-rayed!

The left side of the brain, for example, handles more of the reasoning and mathematical calculation, and enables you to understand grammar and recognize words when you learn a language. If certain parts of your left hemisphere are damaged, you become unable to speak or form words.

The right side, however, is used more in interpreting the *sounds* and *emotions* of language and speech. It is used more in listening to music. And it also deals better with visual information, like recognizing faces and facial expressions. There's also some evidence that the right half of the brain is more developed (and used) in artists and musicians.

But while the two sides of your brain may specialize in slightly different things, what's really important is how they work together and complement each other. Given the choice, your brain likes to coordinate the two halves and split duties between them. But as we've already learned, if you only have one half left to work with, your brain can still make do. It just takes time for the brain to rewire itself, so that it can handle most or all of the jobs it was doing before.

So when my teacher tells me to 'use my brain', can I ask her which half?
Well, you could try it. But nobody likes a smarty-pants. Even one with half a brain . . .

What happens in your head during a headache?

That depends on what's causing it. Headaches can be caused by any number of different things going on inside your bonce – including pinched nerves, tight blood vessels and swollen brain membranes. But, while your brain receives and interprets pain signals, it can't actually feel pain at all. Brain pain is a funny thing . . .

Wait – what? Brains don't feel any pain?

That's right, they don't. For the most part, pain starts at the tips of sensory nerves spread throughout your body. There are sensory nerves tied to pain receptors on your skin, which send signals to the brain when your skin is pinched, scraped, burned, cut or pierced. There are sensory nerves tied to your muscles and tendons, which send pain signals to the brain when you stretch or pull them too hard. And there are sensory nerves running alongside blood vessels throughout your body, which send pain signals to the brain when your tissues and organs are bumped, squashed, cut or punctured.

But the inside of the brain itself contains no sensory nerve endings at all. So it can't feel any pain. None at all. In fact, when brain surgeons operate on tumours and brain lesions, they sometimes leave the patient awake while they do it!

Yikes! Really?

Yep, it's true. Since cutting through the skin and skull *would* be painful, the patient is usually given a local anaesthetic to kill the pain at the surface. But once the 'lid' is off (so to speak), the surgeon can slice and dice away at the brain itself while *chatting* to the wide-awake patient!

That's kind of freaky.

A little bit, yes.

Okay, so if headaches don't actually happen inside your brain, then why does it *feel* like they do?

Because the cause of the headache is often still inside your *head* – just not inside the brain itself. Your brain, after all, isn't the only thing inside your skull. Between your brain and your skull, there are three layers of fatty* membranes called **meninges** (these are the things that get infected if you have **meningitis**). They contain a vast web of blood vessels which brings oxygen and nutrients to the hungry brain below, and envelop the brain in a protective triple-bag of fat and **cerebrospinal fluid**. (Picture a grey, fatty lasagne on top of your cauliflower-like brain and you're not far off.)

---

* Yep, no matter how healthy your body is, your brain is *fat*. The average brain is about 60 per cent fat, with most of the rest being water.

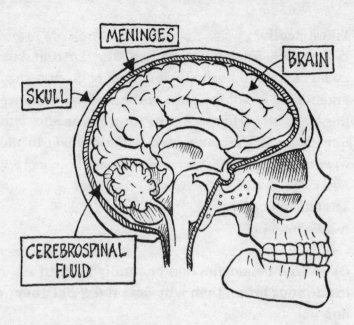

MENINGES

BRAIN

SKULL

CEREBROSPINAL
FLUID

Anyway, it's *these* surrounding areas – not the brain itself – that are most often the cause of headaches. Most often, headaches are caused by pinched or narrowed blood vessels within the meninges. As the blood pressure builds up behind the pinch, the vessel walls get stretched, and pain receptors in the walls signal the brain to say there's a problem.

But what makes *that* happen? I mean, if headaches are so common, those blood vessels must get pinched all the time, right?
Well, there are over 100,000 miles of blood vessels surrounding the brain (enough, if you unwound them all, to wrap right round the Earth four times!). So there's plenty of room for pinches and swellings

to happen *somewhere* in there. And there are *lots* of different ways they can get pinched and swollen.

Like what?
The simplest way is if you bump your head. Do this hard enough, and it will crush or bust open small blood vessels surrounding the brain, causing a painful headache. (Bust or crush enough of them, and you can end up with brain damage – all the more reason to wear a helmet if you're on a bike or skateboard.)

If you don't drink enough water and become **dehydrated**, an entire membrane can shrink as it loses water, squeezing blood vessels inside and causing another type of headache. On the flipside, if you drink *too much* water (which is called **hyperhydration**), your whole brain can swell up and press against the membranes, causing yet *another* type of headache. Other common causes for headaches include

- pulled or stiff neck muscles – these pinch nerves and blood vessels in the back of the head
- eye strain – nerve pain from overworked muscles that control your eye movements. Again, these nerves are close enough to the brain for it to confuse it with 'brain pain'.
- respiratory and sinus infections – the viruses that cause colds, flu and other respiratory diseases can infect your nasal passages and sinuses, causing swelling of the membranes inside. These then press on nerves and blood vessels behind the eyes, nose

and forehead, causing painful 'pressure' or 'sinus' headaches until the infection is fought off.

• alcohol, drugs, medicines, stress, air pressure changes and allergies to certain foods, all of which cause swelling in the blood vessels of the meninges . . . and, of course, sudden heat loss from the roof of the mouth caused by eating frozen foods too fast – which causes the nerves above to shrink up. This gives a lovely 'behind-the-eye' headache . . . better known as 'brain freeze' or 'ice-cream headache'. But at least that one's easily avoided.

How, by taking aspirin or something?
Errr . . . no. You *could* just eat your ice cream more slowly . . .

Oh, right. I knew that.

Experiment: send more blood to your brain!

No, I'm not going to make you stand on your head. This is all about showing how your brain demands more blood flow (to get more glucose and oxygen) the more you put it to work.

Remember the heartbeat experiment back in Chapter 5? Well this time, you're going to find the heartbeat in your throat, in one of the main arteries leading to the brain. Here's how you do it:

1) Place two fingers (lightly) along the side of your throat, just beneath the jaw and to one side of the middle. Press down gently until you feel your pulse beating in the artery beneath.
2) Relax, and measure your heartbeats per minute using a stopwatch (or get a friend to time it while you count beats), just as we did before. Note the number down.
3) Now get your friend to place his fingers on your throat, in the same place you had yours. Once they've checked they can feel it, have them start the timer and count how many times your pulse beats for you.
4) In that one minute, try to think of as many different animal species as you can – cats, dogs, iguanas, ostriches – you name it. Even dinosaurs, if you like. Just keep going, and see if you can

think of at least thirty of them. Don't stop thinking!

5) Now have your friend tell you what your heart rate for that frantic thinking minute was. Compare it with the 'resting, relaxed' rate from before. Chances are it was much higher the second time, as thinking hard actually redirects blood to your hungry brain! Believe it or not, thinking is *hard* work!

What's the highest IQ you can get?

The highest IQ measured to date is 210. Which is pretty much as high as you can possibly get on the test. Most people score close to 100, but your IQ changes as you age and train your brain, so it's worth taking the test more than once! And remember: 'IQ' is not the same as 'intelligence'.

It isn't? But I thought IQ was a measure of your intelligence?

Not quite. The **Intelligence Quotient** (or IQ), scored using a standardized IQ test, is not a direct measure of intelligence. It's a measure of *relative* intelligence.

What's the difference?

A direct measurement is one you make using a independent scale – like a tape measure for height, or a set of bathroom scales for weight. These scales give absolute measures, like 150 cm, 90 kg, 5ft 8in, 10 stone, and so on.

But a relative measure is different. A relative measure of height, for example, might compare your height with that of everyone else your age. So let's say the average height for a ten-year-old is 4ft, 8in. We could then give that average height a score of 100 (as in 100 per cent).

So if you were 4ft 6in tall, your *relative height* (compared to the average ten-year-old) would be

96 per cent of the average, or 96. And here are a few more relative measures, on the same scale:

3ft = 64	4ft = 85	4ft 10in = 103	5ft 5in = 115
3ft 7in = 78	4ft 2in = 89	5ft = 107	6ft = 128

Now we can look at the range of relative heights, and pick out a smaller range around the average (let's say, 85–115, that we call 'normal height' for a ten-year-old. Anything below 85, we could call 'short', and anything above 115, we call 'tall'.

So on this relative height scale, we'd expect *most* ten-year-olds to measure between 4ft and 5ft 5in tall. Anyone below 4ft, we'd say was 'short for their age'. And any ten-year-old measuring over 5ft 5in, we'd say was 'tall for their age'. Get it?

Got it.
Well, that's more or less how IQ works. Since intelligence (like height) develops with age, it's kind of pointless to give a five-year-old the same IQ test as a ten-year-old and declare the winner 'more intelligent'. The ten-year-old has a five-year headstart, and has learned lots more things, so you wouldn't be surprised if the ten-year-old scored much higher.

Instead, five-year-olds are tested and compared to other five-year-olds, while ten-year-olds are compared to other ten-year-olds. Then an average score and a 'normal' range is calculated for each group, giving a scale of relative intelligence. Once again, 85–115 is the 'average' range of intelligence on each scale, while anything above 115 is considered 'above average' and anything below 85 'below average'.

This, really, is what the IQ test was created for. It wasn't so adults could see how much cleverer they were compared to other people. It was to check whether children were developing normal intelligence for their age.

So what's a good score, and what's a bad score?

Well, here's the scoring scale for one of the original IQ tests. (Modern ones tend to be a bit more tactful and generous with the scores, but you get the idea.)

Over 140	genius or near-genius
120–140	very superior intelligence
110–119	superior intelligence
90–109	average or normal intelligence
80–89	dullness
70–79	borderline deficiency in intelligence
Under 70	feeble-mindedness

So who has the highest ever IQ? Has anyone ever totally aced the test?

The highest ever IQ on record belongs to South Korean physicist and engineer Kim Ung-yong, who once scored 210. Anything over 200 is usually declared 'unmeasurable' on an adult IQ test, which gives you some idea of how bright this guy really is. (In fact, he learned advanced mathematics at age three, was speaking several languages by age four, and graduated from Colorado State University with a PhD in Physics before turning fifteen!)

Other notable clever-heads are chess champion **Garry Kasparov** (said to have an IQ of over 190) and the famous physicists **Stephen Hawking** (above) and **Albert Einstein** (below) – both with IQs of over 160.

So, if you have bigger brain, do you have a bigger IQ?

Not necessarily, no. Although Einstein *did* have an unusually large brain, neuroscientists (scientists who study the brain and nervous system) have revealed

that people with high IQs generally have the same-sized brains as everyone else. As far as the brain goes, it's not the size, but the *wiring* that makes you more or less intelligent.

How's that, then?

Your brain contains millions of individual brain cells (or neurons). And each neuron makes between ten and a hundred connections with other neurons within the brain. As your brain grows and develops, more and more of these connections are formed, and by the time you're an adult there are *trillions* of connections buzzing away inside your head. It's these connections – not simply the swelling of your brain to a larger size – that increase your intelligence as you age.

So are super-intelligent people born with super-connected brains?

That seems to be part of it, yes. But since your brain makes new connections every time you learn something, your network of connections – and your intelligence – can also be developed by learning. As far as we can work out, for most people, about 50 per cent of your IQ comes from genes and inborn intelligence you inherit from your parents, while the other 50 per cent comes from learning, experience and brain-training.

So you're not just born clever? You can *learn* to be intelligent too?

Absolutely. In fact, it's fairly easy to increase your IQ with learning and practice. And while you might never score as high as Kim Ung-yong, there's no doubt that you'll be a cleverer person after studying.

It's also worth noting that while an IQ score can give you some idea of how 'intelligent' you are, it isn't an absolute measure of what we call 'intelligence'. People who score high on IQ tests typically have good memories, are good at acquiring new knowledge and have good logical reasoning skills. But intelligence is also about adapting to and learning from your environment, understanding relationships and emotions, and thinking creatively. These things aren't fully tested in IQ tests, so people with these kinds of intelligence can score lower on tests, even though they are still very intelligent people.

Many clever anthropologists (scientists who study people) living with native tribes in Borneo and Brazil have been alarmed to discover that the people they studied thought them rather stupid. Everyone in the tribe could, for example, walk for miles into thick jungle, and still find their way home without a map or compass. Clever as they were, the scientists often missed the clues and cues that would allow them to do the same, and wandered around lost for hours before being found.

Though these tribespeople might score lower on a standard IQ test, it would be hard to say they were 'less able to learn from their environment' than the scientists. So who, really, is more intelligent? Often, it's hard to say. It depends where you are, and what you're trying to do.

Okay – one last thing. Do boys have higher IQs than girls?

That's a tricky one. Some studies say yes, while others say that, on average, there's no difference at all. I'll leave you to argue that one with your friends. In the meantime, have a go at the IQ test questions below. They might help you settle the argument!

Quick IQ test

*See how clever and quick-witted you are with this simple IQ test. (Note that this isn't a proper, full IQ test, but it'll give you some idea of what taking a timed IQ test is like). Answer **T** (True) or **F** (False). You have only five minutes. Answers on page 235.*

1) A pizza can be divided into more than seven pieces by making four cuts.

2) Two of the following numbers add up to thirteen: 1, 6, 3, 5, 11

3) If written backwards, the number, 'one thousand, one hundred twenty-five,' would be written 'five thousand, two hundred eleven.'

4) The letters of the word, 'sponged,' appear in reverse alphabetical order.

5) If Monday is the first day of the month, the very next Saturday is the fifth day of the month.

6) Fred will be four miles from his starting place if he travels two miles north, then three miles east, and then two miles south.

227

Why can't you taste things when your nose is bunged up?

Because many of the things we think we're tasting we're actually smelling instead. The chemical sensors in your nose are much more sensitive than those on your tongue. So when the ones in your nose are blocked off, you're left with a much weaker sense, and only very strong-tasting foods can be recognized.

That's just silly. How could you confuse a smell with a taste?

Because our senses of smell and taste are very similar. They both rely on special proteins, called **chemoreceptors**, which recognize certain chemicals in the air or in our food. In the nose, these receptors are clustered on a little coin-sized patch called the **olfactory mucosa**, high up inside the nose. On the tongue, the receptors are on the surface of **taste cells**, which are clustered into thousands of tiny **taste buds** that cover the bumps and ridges of the tongue.

When these receptors recognize a specific chemical, they send a message to the brain via nerve signals. The brain then pieces together that information and compares it to memories of similar signals it has received from the nose and tongue in the past. If it finds a match, the brain then *creates* the sensation of taste or smell inside your mind, whether it's 'beefburger', 'boiled sprout', 'chocolate', 'coffee', 'vanilla ice cream' or whatever.

But tastes and smells are totally different!
How do you mean?

Well, it's not like you can smell a sprout by licking it. Or taste a chocolate bar by shoving it up your nose.
That's true – tastes and smells are different. But because of the close relationship between the two senses, we often confuse the taste of something with its smell. Take chocolate, for example. What does it taste like?

Sweet and chocolatey. And if it's dark chocolate, maybe a little bitter.
Okay, good. Now what does chocolate *smell* like?

Errr . . . well . . . like *chocolate*.
Right. Now here's a fun little experiment for you:

Experiment: choc task

Buy a bar of light chocolate and a bar of dark chocolate. (If possible, find the same brand so that the shape and size is the same and only the flavour is different). Now get a friend to blindfold you and feed you chunks of each one at random. You can repeat this test as often as necessary – all in the name of science, of course! As you do this, try to answer the following two questions:

1) Can you tell the difference between light and dark chocolate without tasting it? (Sniff a couple of chunks without tasting them – can you tell which is which by smell alone?)
2) Can you tell the difference by taste alone, without smell? Hold your nose as you eat a couple of chunks – can you tell which is 'light' and which is 'dark' now?

Try this now, then come back . . .

So how did it go?

Well, from the smell alone, they both just smelled like chocolate and it was hard to tell the difference. When I had my nose plugged up, it tasted funny, but I could taste the difference – one was sweeter and the other more bitter.

Right – so there you have it. Chocolate *smells* **chocolatey**, but *tastes* **sweet** or **bitter**. The same goes for coffee, garlic and lots of other things. Without smell, the *taste* of these things is pretty much reduced to some combination of 'bitter', 'sweet', 'sour' or 'salty'. This is because these are basically the only four* tastes the receptors on your taste buds can pick out. But the *smell* of chocolate, coffee and garlic is much more unique, and this is most of what we're detecting when we recognize their 'flavours'.

But why would your sense of smell be stronger than your sense of taste?

Good question.

Basically, smell is more sensitive than taste because while your tongue only bears *four* different types of chemoreceptors, your nose contains over 400 different types. With these, the average human nose can detect over 10,000 different aromas – everything from 'cedar wood' and 'orange blossom' to 'dead fish' and 'dog poo'.

This, of course, explains why your sense of smell is more powerful *now*, but it doesn't explain *how* it came to be so. That comes down to evolution. Back when our animal ancestors were still swimming around in the ocean, taste and smell used to be the same thing. Even today, fish and other marine animals have one 'sniffing/tasting' sense they use to detect the chemical traces of plants, plankton, predators and prey in the water.

It was only when animals moved on to the *land* – and into the open air – that our senses of smell and

---

* In fact, there's also a fifth taste, called **umami** (from the Japanese word meaning 'deliciousness'). This is a little weaker than the other four tastes, but you might call it 'savoury'.

taste became separated. After that, 'smell' became the ability to detect chemicals in the air, at a distance. For this, you need powerful, sensitive receptors in your nose. (For most land animals, smell is more important than sight or hearing. Only **primates** like monkeys, lemurs, apes and humans depend, first and foremost, on their vision. Smell allows land animals to locate food, find mates, avoid predators and more.

Meanwhile, *taste* became a kind of last-minute check that the food we'd found was nutritious, and not rotten or toxic. Salty and sweet tastes indicate foods rich in nutritious sugars and minerals, while bitter and sour tastes warn us that foods might be rotten or poisonous. In combination, our senses of smell and taste allow us to recognize foods that we might want to eat (or avoid!) if we find them again. But because smell must help us detect those foods *at a distance* – rather than when they're already in your mouth – smell is the more sensitive of the two senses.

Cool! Right – I think I'll repeat that chocolate experiment.
Again?

Only this time, I'll get someone to hide the chocolate all over the house. Then I sniff it out, and scoff it all!
Sounds like fun. Unless, of course, you have a dog. Since dogs have 10,000 times more receptors in their

noses than humans, that'll be a very quick contest.

Plus it'll make a serious, chocolatey mess on the sofa. Hmmm, maybe I'll put him outside first . . .

Answers

p22 Puzzle: blood-clot boggle

C, A, D, E, B

p74 Puzzle: diet and digestion wordsearch

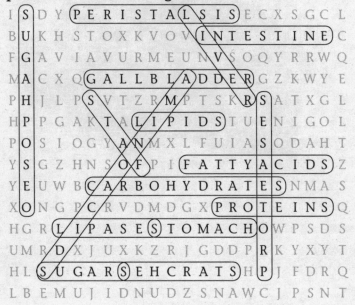

p128 Crossword puzzle: microbes and immunity

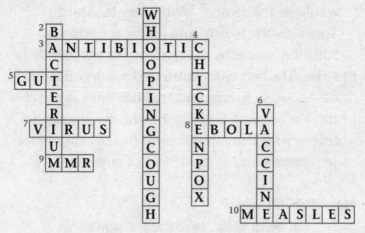

p173 Experiment: bendy bones

The chicken bone becomes very bendy and flexible, almost like rubber! This is because you used the vinegar (otherwise known as acetic acid) to dissolve away all the chalky minerals that gave the bone its hardness, leaving only the rubbery, gel-like tissue behind. Nice work!

p227 Quick IQ test

1) **True**. Four cuts across the diameter of a circular pizza creates eight slices, which is more than seven.

2) **False**. No pair of numbers in that list will add up to thirteen, sorry.

3) **True**. 1125 backwards is 5211.

4) **True**. In reverse order, it reads D-E-G-N-O-P-S.

5) **False**. If Monday is the first day, then Tuesday would be the second, Wednesday the third, Thursday the fourth, and Friday the fifth. So Saturday would be the sixth day of the month.

6) **False**. The two miles north and south cancel each other out, so in effect all Fred has done is travel three miles east. If you're having trouble seeing this in your head, just draw it (using centimetres to represent miles) on a piece of paper.

How did you score?

1–2   Oh dear. Better take the test again (or pretend you didn't).

3–4   Impressive. Bordering on brilliance.

5–6   Genius. If Einstein was alive, he'd be trying to copy your maths homework.

(Test taken from www.iqtest.com)

Picture Credits
Illustrations by Mike Phillips, except:

page 4 Kingfisher
page 224 (top) Science Museum; (bottom) NMPFT/
Daily Herald Archive.

Index

Space, black holes and stuff

Glenn Murphy

What is a black hole?

How do we know that stars and galaxies are billions of years old?

What is the difference between stars and planets?

Packed with information about all sorts of incredible things like supermassive black holes, galaxies, telescopes, planets, solar flares, constellations, eclipses and red dwarfs, this book has no boring bits!

SCIENCE SORTED

Evolution, nature and stuff

Glenn Murphy

How did we develop from chemical soup into internet-surfing human beings?

What is a selfish gene?

What are the kingdoms of life?

Evolution and genetics are like a map for exploring the whole world of living things. Trace the history of life right back to our earliest ancestors and you'll be amazed at what you find. This book tells you everything you need to know, with none of the boring bits!